Totalitarianism

Leonard Schapiro
London School of Economics and Political Science

Pall Mall · London

The Pall Mall Press
5 Cromwell Place, London SW7

First published 1972
© 1972 by The Pall Mall Press
ISBN 0 269 02706 8

Printed in Great Britain by
The Garden City Press Limited
Letchworth, Hertfordshire

Contents

5/How Useful Is the Concept? 99

'Key Concepts'
an Introductory Note

Political concepts are part of our daily speech—we abuse 'bureaucracy' and praise 'democracy', welcome or recoil from 'revolution'. Emotive words such as 'equality', 'dictatorship', 'élite' or even 'power' can often, by the very passions which they raise, obscure a proper understanding of the sense in which they are, or should be, or should not be, or have been used. Confucius regarded the 'rectification of names' as the first task of government. 'If names are not correct, language will not be in accordance with the truth of things', and this in time would lead to the end of justice, to anarchy and to war. One could with some truth point out that the attempts hitherto by governments to enforce their own quaint meanings on words have not been conspicuous for their success in the advancement of justice. 'Rectification of names' there must certainly be: but most of us would prefer such rectification to take place in the free debate of the university, in the competitive arena of the pages of the book or journal.

Analysis of commonly used political terms, their reassessment or their 'rectification', is, of course, normal activity in the political science departments of our universities. The idea of this series was indeed born in the course of discussion between a few university teachers of political science, of whom Professor S. E. Finer of Manchester University was one. It occurred to us that a series of short books, discussing the 'Key Concepts' in political science would serve two purposes. In universities these books could provide the kind of brief political texts which might be of assistance to students in gaining a fuller understanding of the terms which they were constantly using. But we also hoped that outside the universities there exists a reading public which has the time, the curiosity and the inclination to pause to reflect on some of those words and ideas which are so often taken for granted. Perhaps even 'that insidious and crafty animal', as Adam Smith described the politican and statesman, will occasionally derive some pleasure or even profit from that more leisurely analysis which academic study can afford, and which a busy life in the practice of politics often denies.

It has been very far from the minds of those who have been concerned in planning and bringing into being the 'Key Concepts' series to try and impose (as if that were possible!) any uniform pattern on the authors who have contributed, or will contribute, to it. I, for one, hope that each author will, in his own individual manner, seek and find the best way of helping us to a fuller understanding of the concept which he has chosen to analyse. But whatever form the individual exposition may take, there are, I believe, three aspects of illumination which we can confidently expect from each volume in this series. First, we can look for some examination of the history of the concept, and of its evolution against a changing social and political background. I believe, as many do who are concerned with the study of political science, that it is primarily in history that the explanation must be sought for many of the perplexing problems of political analysis and judgement which beset us today. Second, there is the semantic aspect. To look in depth at a 'key concept' necessarily entails a study of the name which attached itself to it; of the different ways in which, and the different purposes for which, the name was used; of the way in which in the course of history the same name was applied to several concepts, or several names were applied to one and the same concept; and, indeed, of the changes which the same concept, or what appears to be the same concept, has undergone in the course of time. This analysis will usually require a searching examination of the relevant literature in order to assess the present stage of scholarship in each particular field. And thirdly, I hope that the reader of each volume in this series will be able to decide for himself what the proper and valid use should be of a familiar term in politics, and will gain, as it were, from each volume a sharper and better-tempered tool of political analysis.

There are many today who would disagree with Bismarck's view that politics can never be an exact science. I express no opinion on this much debated question. But all of us who are students of politics—and our numbers both inside and outside the universities continue to grow—will be the better for knowing what precisely we mean when we use a common political term.

London School of Economics
and Political Science

Leonard Schapiro
General Editor

to

Michael Oakeshott

Acknowledgements

This essay is the product of many years' reflection and discussion, in which I have continuously profited from the wisdom of others. Many years ago Professor Julius Gould and I ran a seminar at the London School of Economics and Political Science on Totalitarianism. From the papers and discussions at that seminar I derived my first ideas on this difficult subject. Later, as a Visiting Fellow of the Australian National University, Canberra, I was given the opportunity of conducting some seminars on Totalitarianism. Some time after I was offered the opportunity of conducting a seminar on this topic at the Hebrew University of Jerusalem. I learned a great deal from the participants at all these seminars. If I cannot thank any individuals by name this is due to the fact that the absorption of knowledge and the formulation of ideas is a gradual and imperceptible process, in the course of which the debt to individuals becomes impossible to discern. In the same way, no one who has had the privilege of being a member of the Department of Government at the London School of Economics and Political Science can fail (unless he resolutely rejects social contact with his fellows in the Senior Common Room) to learn constantly from conversation and from criticism. Perhaps I have learned even more from discussions over the years with my students. I do not know to whom specifically my gratitude should be recorded. I hope that all those from whom I have derived so much enlightenment will accept this acknowledgement as the best which I can offer.

I am particularly grateful to my colleagues Maurice Cranston and Ken Minogue, who have read all or part of the manuscript and given me salutary critical comment. I am especially indebted to Michael Oakeshott who gave me his comments on an earlier article in which the substance of what I have to say in this essay first appeared. My wife, Dr Isabel de Madariaga, brought her penetrating intellect and wide historical culture to bear on the manuscript, and gave me the benefit of her critical judgement. To all these I am deeply grateful, though I alone bear the responsibility for the final version. Mrs Helen Burroughs gave me most valuable help in the preparation of the bibliography; and Mrs Ann Kennedy reduced the chaos of a manuscript to the perfection of a typescript. I owe them both a great debt. Mr Bernard G. Mullins, the Editor of 'Key Concepts' for the Pall Mall Press went through the manuscript with the critical appraisal of an experienced and skilled editor, and I owe him my appreciation for many suggestions which I was pleased to adopt.

The literature on totalitarianism is now enormous. I have tried to acknowledge the debt to others where I was aware of it. I am sure that there are many cases where I have borrowed from others without being consciously aware of it, and I can only hope that my fellow scholars in this field will charitably recognize that much of one's reading passes into one's unconscious, and that failure to acknowledge a debt is not due to any deliberate omission.

London School of Economics and Political Science
1 March 1972

1/Introduction

The history of a word

The word 'totalitarian' appears to have originated in Italy
(according to some authorities it came into the Italian language
from the French, though the French philological dictionaries claim
that it reached the French language from the Italian). Mussolini's
first use of the word was in a speech on June 22, 1925 in which, in
attacking the remnants of the opposition in the Chamber, he spoke
of 'la nostra feroce volontà totalitaria'.[1] ('Our'—*scilicet* the Fascists'
—'fierce totalitarian will'.)

But Mussolini did not invent the word. The philosopher
Giovanni Gentile, who was to become the official philosopher of
Fascist theory, had also spoken of Fascism as 'a total conception of
life' in a speech of March 8 of the same year.[2] On the other hand,
liberal opponents of Fascism, around the same time, were using the
word as a term of opprobrium for dictatorial and dishonest political
practices.[3] In the course of the next few years, the word became a
favourite term in Mussolini's vocabulary, used to describe the system which he claimed to have created, and which he usually called
'lo stato totalitario', the 'totalitarian state'. In the official exposition
of Fascist doctrine, written as to the first part by Gentile, and as to
the second by Mussolini, the word appears in each part—the first
part applies it to 'Fascism', the second to the way of government
pursued by the Fascist Party.[4]

In Germany, the use of the term *total* or *totalitär* by the
National Socialists was short-lived. It was apparently first used in
the military sense of 'total mobilization' by Ernst Juenger in 1930.
In the following year Carl Schmitt, a lawyer who was shortly to
become one of the main ideologists of National Socialism, discussed
the National Socialist idea of the 'totalitarian state'.[5] Hitler seldom
used the word and then normally with the pre-fix 'so-called'. His

13

own favourite word was *autoritär* which he used constantly—it was a word full of resonances likely to appeal to a German audience. In the early years of National Socialist power *totalitär* was used by some National Socialist leaders, but it soon fell into disuse, no doubt in deference to Hitler who perhaps did not wish to stress, by implication, any ideological debt to Mussolini on the part of National Socialism.[6]

In Soviet Russia, according to the *Dictionary of the Soviet Academy*, it was used in 1940 and thereafter, and applied exclusively to 'Fascist' régimes. Official Soviet writers strongly deprecate the use of the term 'totalitarian' as applied by non-Soviet writers to the Soviet régime, and contend that this is an aspect of 'cold war' propaganda. On the other hand, the term is frequently applied to the Soviet régime in the very extensive secretly disseminated writings by members of various dissent movements which have been circulating in the Soviet Union in past years. The first officially recorded use in English, according to the *Oxford English Dictionary* (Supplement Volume), was in an article in the *Quarterly Review* in 1928. (Actually the word 'totalitarian' was used in an English translation, published in 1926, of Luigi Sturzo, *Italy and Fascismo*.) In the same year as its appearance in England, 1928, the word 'totalitarian', in the general sense of 'all-embracing', or comprehensive, as applied to Fascist doctrine, was used twice by Giovanni Gentile in an article in the American journal *Foreign Affairs*.[7] In 1929, the word appeared in a leading article in *The Times*, where it was applied to both National Socialist Germany and Communist Russia, and contrasted with 'parliamentary' governments. In American usage thereafter and before the Second World War the word was variously applied either to Fascist Italy and National Socialist Germany, or to those two countries and the Soviet Union. For example, G. H. Sabine, in his article on 'The State' in the 1934 edition of the *Encyclopaedia of the Social Sciences* applied the term to one-party states, including the USSR. Some other political scientists up to 1941 also applied the term to the three states concerned. But there were some who drew a sharp distinction between the Soviet and Fascist types of rule, and reserved the term 'totalitarian' for the latter alone: the same distinction was drawn by Webster's *International Dictionary* in its edition of 1939.

Since the end of the war the use of the word 'totalitarian' by journalists, politicians and writers on politics has become widespread, indiscriminate and imprecise. It has been applied to a great variety of political régimes: to the Soviet Union, to National Socialist Germany and Fascist Italy, as well as to the many régimes which have sprung up in imitation of them, or as a result of imposition by force of Soviet-dominated Communist Party rule—China since 1949, for example, Cuba or the People's Democracies of Eastern Europe. It has also been applied to Russia under the Czars, to India during the Mauryu dynasty, to the Roman Empire in the reign of Diocletian, to Plato's ideal Republic, to China, both contemporary and in the Ch'in Dynasty, to the United States both in the 1960s and the 1840s, to ancient Sparta, to Meiji Japan, to Geneva under Calvin and to the Catholic Church—among many others. The term has been applied to 'movements', 'parties', 'leaders', 'processes', 'ideals' and 'syntax'.[8] We have also had 'totalitarian crushing policies' from General de Gaulle, and 'the totalitarian universe of technological rationality' from Herbert Marcuse.[9] As the Russians say—'Paper will stand anything'.

The question of method

This short history of the term already shows the need for an appraisal of the sense or senses in which its usage may be justified. This examination, to which the remainder of this essay will be devoted, seems to require a number of stages. The first stage is to examine the main features or contours of the three countries to which the term was in fact applied, mainly in the decade between 1930 and 1940, when the word 'totalitarian' was taking root in the English language, in Great Britain and in the United States. This examination will make it possible to establish the essential and characteristic features of the three societies concerned: Italy during the ascendancy of Mussolini, Germany under the rule of Hitler, and the Soviet Union under the rule of Stalin.

It should be observed at the outset that special considerations apply to the Soviet Union. In both Italy and Germany the régimes created were the work of one man, who in each case conquered power, survived for a time, and then fell as the result of defeat in war. In the case of Russia, Stalin inherited the power which had been conquered by Lenin; and changes have taken place in the Soviet Union since Stalin's death in 1953. The search for common features within the three régimes must therefore, in the Soviet case, be confined to the Stalin era, leaving open for further discussion in its proper context the question whether the term 'totalitarian' is applicable either to Soviet Russia in the early years of its history or in the years which have elapsed since 1953. Thus, there are those who contend that whatever may be said about Stalin's régime, that which existed under Lenin, and for some years after his death while the New Economic Policy lasted, was not 'totalitarianism'. Others maintain that whatever may be true with regard to Stalin's régime the USSR should not be described as totalitarian today. These are important and interesting questions, but they need not arise so long as our consideration is for the present limited to the period of Stalin's power.

Having once established the salient features or contours of the three prototypes,* it will be possible to proceed to the examination of the main questions which are the subject of controversy in the very extensive literature which has grown up on the subject of 'totalitarianism'. Among such questions are the following: Should one term be used for the three political systems, or are Communism and Fascism so different that no one term can properly embrace them both? To what polities can the term be applied? Is Spain totalitarian, for example? And, if not, then where does the distinction lie? Is the form of rule under discussion—as distinct from the name—new? There is also the question of change: a description which is valid when first applied may become obsolete through change. Yet, from force of habit or from lack of meticulous care in the use of language, the old term may continue to be applied. For example, there have been substantial developments, not all equally far-reaching, in almost all the Communist states since 1953. Even if they could properly be described as 'totalitarian' in the past, can they still be so described in 1972 with any accuracy?

These are important questions, but to attempt to answer them is not to conclude the examination of the concept. For the concept of

* See p. 99 for justification for the use of this term.

'totalitarianism' may have existed in the minds of men long before Mussolini adopted, and tempted us to use, this word—as ugly and pretentious as his architecture. Moreover, such ideas in past ages could have influenced the men who shaped the modern political systems which we have to discuss. A study of the *concept* of 'totalitarianism', as reflected in the history of political thought (long before the *word* was invented) is therefore also a necessary part of this enquiry. (Much of the literature on 'totalitarianism' is concerned with analysis of the social conditions which led to the emergence of particular political systems. But such enquiry, though of enormous interest and importance, is only indirectly of relevance to the enquiry which will be pursued in these pages.)

It should perhaps be observed that the statement of the problem outlined above is by no means universally accepted. Professor F. J. Fleron Jr, for example, who has devoted a great deal of thought to the question of the relevance of 'totalitarianism' as a concept applicable to Communist régimes, takes a very different view. In a recent study in which he cogently argues the need for concepts other than 'totalitarianism' when dealing with the Communist countries today, he draws attention to the wide variety of meanings that different writers attach to 'totalitarianism' and urges greater precision in delimiting this term. For, he says, 'without proper denotation of the concept, we do not know what systems to study and observe'.[10] This seems to me to be an inversion of the proper order: we do, in fact, know what systems to study and observe, namely the three countries to which the term was in fact applied in the 1930s. It is from the study of these three alone that proper limits to the use of, and meanings of, the term 'totalitarian' can be discovered. And it is only when once these limits have been discovered that it becomes possible to ask some of the further questions which arise. Is it correct to apply the same terms to Fascist Italy, Nazi Germany and Stalinist Russia? Can this term still validly be applied to any or all of the Communist states today? What other polities, past or present, can it be applied to—if any? This is the method which it is intended to pursue in the pages that follow.[11]

2/Contours and Features of Totalitarianism

The six-point syndrome

The most influential attempt to reduce to order the baffling features which characterize 'totalitarian' régimes was made by Professor Carl J. Friedrich in 1954. As the title of his work ('The Unique Character in Totalitarian Society') showed, his analysis claimed to demonstrate two propositions, both of which have since been widely disputed: that 'totalitarianism' was a new and unique form of political rule; and that its characteristics were common to both the Fascist and the Communist types.[1] Friedrich listed five aspects or factors which he claimed were common to all contemporary totalitarian societies: an official ideology, to which everyone is supposed to adhere, focussed on a 'perfect final state of mankind'; a single mass party usually led by one man, organized hierarchically and either superior to or intertwined with the state bureaucracy; a technically conditioned near-complete monopoly of control, by the party and the bureaucracy subordinate to it, of the effective use of all weapons of armed combat; a near-complete monopoly similarly exercised over all means of effective mass communication; and a system of physical or psychological terroristic police control. This combination of factors, upon which Friedrich based his claim regarding the uniqueness of totalitarian society, in the sense that such a combination of all of them had hitherto been unknown in history, was somewhat enlarged by an important additional sixth factor in a book published (jointly with Z. Brzezinski) in 1956: central control and direction of the entire economy.[2] Some further slight modifications were also made in the following years to the 'six-point syndrome', as it is frequently called—and quite aptly: for a syndrome, in its normal meaning, signifies the concurrence of certain symptoms which together constitute the disease. These modifications were the result both of criticisms and of the changes

18

which had become observable in the Communist countries after 1953.

But basically Professor Friedrich's view remained unaltered, as was made evident in an essay published in 1969, in which he in effect restated the 'six-point syndrome'. He did however add two qualifications to what he had written in 1953. Monopoly of control was now extended by him so as to embrace not only mass communications and weapons but 'all organizations, including economic ones'. This addition was important, since one of the most characteristic features of Communist rule in practice is the way in which no seemingly independent institution or organization, however humble, is allowed to exist unless the ruling élite can maintain some kind of control over it. And secondly, Professor Friedrich now stressed that the monopoly control is 'not necessarily exercised by the party'—as some critics had inferred from his earlier formulation. 'The important point is that such a monopolistic control is in the hands of whatever "élite" rules the particular society and thereby constitutes its régime.'[3] This was also a significant modification, made necessary by further study in recent years of the régimes concerned.

It would require lengthy analysis to list all the criticisms to which the 'syndrome' has been subjected, and to show how the author has dealt with them, but it should be stated at the outset that whatever criticism of detail may be levelled at the Friedrich syndrome, it still dominates nearly every discussion of the question of 'totalitarianism'. Broadly speaking, criticism has been directed along the following two lines. First, there are the critics of detail, who wish to add to or subtract from the six-point syndrome. For example, it has been contended that there are two further factors which are as important as the six: a theory of world domination implied in the official ideology; and the need for constant mass mobilization of effort. From the opposite point of view, it can be (and has been) argued that monopoly of control over effective operational weapons is an essential factor in every government which intends to remain in authority, and is not peculiar to the 'totalitarian' form. The second broad group of critics consists of those who accept the syndrome with or without some modifications or additions, but contend that the uniqueness and novelty inferred from it by its author for the nature of the totalitarian régime cannot be sustained: all these features, it has been argued, can be found elsewhere, in the past or even in the present; and the presence of modern technology, which is an essential element in Friedrich's argument, can produce only a difference of degree, but not a difference of kind.

It is not proposed in the pages which follow to continue the arguments for or against the six-point syndrome, except in so far as some of the arguments may become relevant in another context. The syndrome has done its work: but it is time to escape from it. Valuable as it is, it hampers analysis because it confuses two entirely different things: the characteristic features, or, as I prefer to call them, 'contours' of a polity;[4] and the instruments of rule. Thus, it is an historical fact that all the three prototype régimes originated in a mass movement headed by a powerful leader, and that the mass movements became (in different ways and to a different extent) ruling élites or parties. But the party is merely an instrument of rule: in contrast, the existence and importance of the leader forms a contour without which the three prototypes would be unrecognizable. To put at the head of the syndrome the mass party usually headed by a leader is to confound instrument and contour. Similarly, the monopoly of means of communication or of economic means is a contour, a characteristic feature without which the totalitarian régime would cease to be its distinctive self: party, police, and, as will be seen below, ideology are all means to the end, they are instruments of rule. What is proposed in this chapter is to consider the five contours from which the map reader in the political wilderness will recognize the 'totalitarian' régime: the Leader; the subjugation of the legal order; control over private morality; continuous mobilization; and legitimacy based on mass support. The distinctive instruments or pillars of 'totalitarianism' will then be considered in the next chapter.

The Leader   Pg 3

To anyone looking at the three prototype régimes in the course of the 1930s, the first feature that would strike him would

necessarily be that of the Leader. Mussolini, Stalin, Hitler—all
were elevated by propaganda machinery on a scale unknown in
modern times to a position not only of Leaders, but of Leaders
who were alleged to be endowed with qualities which raised them
far above the level of ordinary men. Those of us who have survived
to the present can, of course, see the bombast, the fraud, the
hysteria and the mass hypnosis which made gods out of sordid
psychopaths and mountebanks; and who in their fall and defeat
(posthumous in the case of Stalin) are revealed as tyrannous and
often incompetent in everything except the art of keeping themselves in power. Both Fascism and National Socialism were essentially the products of the ambition and energy of one man, even if
the one man could not have succeeded except in the circumstances
which time and place offered in order to enable him to snatch at
victory. (Had Hitler been born, say, in a Buckinghamshire village
in 1889 instead of an Austrian village, he would no doubt have
ended on the gallows or in a madhouse.) Stalin, it is true, inherited
from Lenin, at all events in embryonic form, an effective machine
with which to build up his own power: even so, the personal
imprint of Stalin's style is the most distinctive single characteristic
of the Soviet Union after the end of the New Economic Policy in
1928. Each of the three Leaders is on record as having instinctively
recognized his own unique quality. Hitler, for all the talk of the
Thousand Year Reich, proclaimed in private conversation that no
successor worthy of him was imaginable. Mussolini confessed to
Emil Ludwig that in his view there could be no second Duce, and
Stalin (according to Khrushchev) expressed fears of what his suc-
cessors, who were 'as blind as kittens', would do without him. (Of
course, the mania of indispensability can afflict smaller scale
psychopaths than Mussolini, Hitler, or Stalin.)

Leaders of the type of Mussolini, Hitler, and Stalin have frequently, following Max Weber's classic study of the source of the
authority of power, been described as 'charismatic'. The quality of
'charisma' in a leader, according to Weber's analysis, consists in his
apparent possession of 'supernatural or superhuman or at all events
specifically out of the ordinary' qualities, which make him appear
an emissary of God, or a destined Leader. Weber is not concerned

with the objective truth about the Leader's qualities, and is prepared to include frauds and charlatans in his category of 'charismatic' Leaders.[5] To this extent a case can be made out for designating our three 'totalitarian' Leaders as 'charismatic', since, whatever their objective qualities, one cannot deny the extraordinary influence which they could wield at different times over large sections of their fellow countrymen, by means other than rational persuasion.

However there is another element involved which perhaps makes Weber's category less appropriate, at any rate in the cases of Mussolini and Stalin: the methods and process by which each of these three Leaders rose to power and ascendancy. In the case of Mussolini there were his *squadri* (gangs) with the *manganello* (cosh) and the castor oil; Stalin rose through his network of the party and police apparatus. Of the three Leaders, Hitler more than the other two seemed to possess the magnetic qualities which attracted a following right from the start. But even he could never have risen to power without his network of SA gangsters to do the preparatory, 'manipulative' work for him. In each case the 'charisma' was bolstered and supplemented, one is almost tempted to say created, by a long, preparatory process of manipulation in which opponents are terrorized and silenced, in which decisions are taken in advance of the meetings which ostensibly are supposed to take these decisions, and unanimity is simulated by a combination of terror, intrigue and showmanship; and in which the Leader is gradually built up as infallible and invincible.

The case of Stalin illustrates this best. His position after the death of Lenin in 1924 remained very vulnerable: he was challenged by opponents with much better claims than himself to become the new ruler of the country. His defence against this was the patient building up of the network of party officials and delegates bribed and pledged to support him in advance, but still required to preserve the façade of democratic party decision. The climax comes at the Fourteenth Congress of the Party in December 1925. The opposition has already been outmanoeuvred, but the pretence of free debate is still maintained. In the course of his speech one of the opponents, Kamenev, directly attacks Stalin: 'I have come to the conclusion that Comrade Stalin cannot fulfil the role of unifier of the bolshevik general staff ... we are against the doctrine of one-man rule, we are against the creation of a Leader.' (Here we observe two quite distinct political notions in conflict. Kamenev is appealing, possibly in despair, to the Congress as if it were a genuine representative and deliberative body, inviting support for a rational argument, asking for a decision. But two years of manipulation by Stalin have transformed the Congress. It is no longer a forum for debate and decision: it is an instrument for the endorsement of the Leader by ostensible mass support, and nothing more.) Immediately after Kamenev's words pandemonium breaks out: the assembled delegates show their outraged, 'spontaneous' indignation—all carefully recorded in the stenogram of the proceedings. Stalin's lieutenants 'guide the general bedlam into a staged ovation for the General Secretary'.[6] Before long 'Leader' will become the usual title for the man who will amass adulation and power to an extent hitherto unknown in Russia's history. If this is 'charisma' it includes something else as well, and this new element is mass manipulation, which formed no part of Weber's analysis.

The originator of the technique of mass manipulation, in modern times, was Lenin: not only Stalin, but Mussolini certainly and Hitler (through the German Communists) indirectly, learned it from him. Lenin understood how mass support could be harnessed by long, preparatory, manipulative work instead of being left to the chance of 'spontaneity', which could sway a fickle crowd one way or another. Lenin never became (or ever wanted to become) a Leader such as Hitler or Stalin:[7] but in the course of building up his technique of mass manipulation as part of the process of ensuring victory for his party he provided a model for these very different men.

The Leader in these three prototype societies is something quite different from the ruler of a state, however powerful, as will, it is hoped, become apparent as the analysis unfolds. For the present it is important to emphasize what a Leader is not. In the first place he cannot properly be regarded as merely the head of a party which has captured power within the state—though, of course, capture of power is the first move in the game. Once he is in power, the party, or movement, which enabled him to emerge into prominence becomes as much of a potential rival to his own personal power as any other institution such as the law courts, or the state bureaucracy. Mussolini, Hitler and Stalin, each in turn, having used the party in order to come to power, strove to destroy the institutional nature of his party, to subjugate it, to transform it as far as possible from a hierarchical institution with a political life of its own into a band of obedient followers. The aim in each case was to ensure that every party member was dependent for his continued power and influence on the Leader alone, and in no sense on the authority and dignity of the party as an institution, or of his own office within the party. The success with which this subjugation of the party was achieved varied considerably in the three cases.

Mussolini was, of the three Leaders, both the least competent and the least prepared to use ruthless methods. But he enjoyed the advantage that in Fascist theory the party was subordinate to the state of which he made himself *de facto* head: the Fascist Party was defined in its Statute in the version of 1938, as 'a voluntary civil militia under the orders of the Leader and at the service of the Fascist State'.[8] Long before that date Mussolini, in the course of a series of conflicts with his party, had striven to prevent the party from becoming a rival power to himself, and had in the process converted it from a band of enterprising hooligans, which is how it had started, into a band of ineffective careerists, fit to carry out the Duce's dirtier assignments, and for little more. Party secretaries succeeded one the other with great frequency, and were all men of low calibre.[9] This was indeed a natural enough precaution on Mussolini's part, since it was as Leader of the state and not as head of the party that he had achieved supreme power in January 1925; and a *rival party*, if allowed to achieve any independent dignity, could easily have threatened this position as Leader. It was ironical that the Grand Council of the Fascist Party, which Mussolini himself instituted in 1928, played no part whatever throughout its existence until finally in July 1943 it turned on its creator, and drove him from power. But by that time, of course, Mussolini was a defeated and spent force.

Hitler's position was different: on the one hand the party was in theory, as the embodiment of the will of the *Volk*, superior to the state; on the other hand Hitler did not hesitate to use terror on a scale from which Mussolini shrank. The history of the National Socialist Party up to 1933 shows conclusively the extent to which Hitler succeeded in asserting personal loyalty to his own orders as the sole hierarchical principle within the party.[10] After power was won, the Night of the Long Knives of June 30, 1934 and Hitler's pronouncements in the following months left no doubt that the party was to be a strictly disciplined body in which the authority of the Leader would be supreme and unchallengeable.

Stalin, unlike the other two, inherited a party which he had not himself created. Moreover, he faced the serious problem that in Communist ideology supreme authority lay within the party as a whole, as the vanguard of the victorious class, the proletariat; and that the theory of a supreme Leader, of the kind which National Socialism could propagate on the basis of Germanic tradition, or which Mussolini could attempt to bolster with parallels from ancient Rome, has no place at all in Marxist theory. Stalin's struggle against the attempts of the Communist Party to survive as an institution were prolonged and bloody, and culminated in the holocaust of 1936–38 in which over a million party members and the majority of the party hierarchy perished. He achieved, in the end, what Hitler had achieved in a matter of months: it is small wonder that, according to some accounts, Stalin is said to have expressed envious admiration for Hitler's achievement.[11]

Secondly, just as the power of the Leader did not flow from his party, so it cannot be said to have flowed from the power of the state. In other words, the capture of the state in the case of each of the three Leaders was no more than a preliminary to establishing, or attempting to establish, supreme personal power over the state as well as over the party. It need hardly be stressed that the attempt by one man to hold all the strings of power in his own hands in a large country is unlikely to produce competent or efficient government. Yet the myth of the efficiency of the so-called totalitarian régimes is one of the hardest to kill, in spite of the overwhelming evidence which has now accumulated to prove the full extent of the chaos and incompetence which characterized Mussolini's, Hitler's, and Stalin's rule. Propaganda does its job well so long as the trains run to time to impress the naïve visiting statesman.

Mussolini's failure in establishing his personal power was the greatest of the three, for all the bombast and the mouthing. In 1926 Mussolini was prime minister, president of the council, foreign minister, minister of the interior, minister for the corporations, minister for all three service departments, and commander-in-chief of the militia—as well as Leader of the Fascist Party. In practice, power was dispersed in a multiple confusion of subordinate authorities. The much vaunted 'Corporative state' remained largely on paper. The monarchy, the Church, the police, and the army maintained separate existences; neither the Leader nor the state machine, which under the repeated impacts of the Leader's attacks had been rendered impotent, could co-ordinate, let alone direct them. Rhetoric took the place of government, and bombast that of deliberation. As Mussolini told an old and close friend when the end was near: 'If you could only imagine the effort which it has cost me to search for some kind of equilibrium in which the collisions could be avoided between the antagonistic powers which jostle each other —all jealous, and all distrustful of one another: the government, the party, the monarchy, the Vatican, the army, the militia, the prefects . . . the ministers . . . the big monopoly interests. . . . You will understand, my good friend, these things are the indigestion of totalitarianism.'[12] The 'totalitarian state', which in Fascist theory was the supreme authority, was in fact neither 'totalitarian' nor a 'state': it was the chaos and confusion which one man's ambition had brought about, with the help of the mass support which his peculiar gifts of demagogy enabled him to rally.

Hitler's case was very different. Unlike Mussolini his ideology never exalted the state: the state was always recognized as subordinate to the party, though both existed to do the will of the *Volk*. Since the Führer was not only head of the party but also the mystical voice of the German *Volk*, it was comparatively easy for him, granted the conditions of latent German mass hysteria (always more prevalent than in Italy) to build himself up into the position of unique Leader, apart from and above both state and party. The title of 'Führer and Reich Chancellor' was assumed by Hitler after

Hindenburg's death—thus indicating that his authority derived from some source other than the constitution. In practice this was intended to signify that the authority of the Führer derived neither from the state nor from the party, but from the 'united will of the people': he could act through established state institutions or not, as he wished; he could follow the law or disregard it, or make new law—for the constitutional lawyers of the Third Reich this was all perfectly legally valid authority. It was to the Führer, and him alone, that the soldiers swore allegiance; in practice much earlier and officially by 1944, the title of Reich Chancellor was dropped, and decrees issued in the name of the Führer alone. Yet the state machine, and for that matter the Weimar Constitution, remained in being, side by side with what was variously described as the 'prerogative', or 'ideological' side. This prerogative power derived from the Emergency Ordinance of February 28, 1933, enacted the day after the Reichstag fire: it was only after the outbreak of war that even the pretence of maintaining the legal structure of the state in being was abandoned.[13] In short, like Mussolini but with much greater success, Hitler remained the supreme (if erratic) arbiter among conflicting authorities—state, party and SS, army, and industry,—but, in the last resort, ruthless master of them all.

And herein lies the essence of the Leader in the 'totalitarian' polity: for the Leader to permit a rival *institution*, whether it be the party or the state bureaucracy, or for that matter the army, to maintain any kind of secure existence or independence in relation to him is to run a serious risk of overthrow. Hitler, in his 'Tabletalk', frequently laid stress on the superiority of the 'Leader State' (*Führerstaat*) over any other. Apparently what he meant by this was that the Leader, after his election or choice by acclamation, acquired the kind of supreme authority which could not in any circumstances be challenged on legal or other grounds because he then embodied the will of the people. Such 'Leader states', he argued, 'could last for centuries'—and he cited the example of Venice. Monarchy, with its legal order, presumably, could never last—this, according to Hitler, was Mussolini's trouble: he had failed to erect a *Führerstaat* in which the Leader had 'absolute authority'.[14]

Stalin understood very well the danger of rival institutions. The 'political formula' of the Soviet Union (to use Mosca's phrase) naturally did not permit of any official exaltation of the Leader, who remained the humble General Secretary of the Communist Party. (However, some ingenious Soviet ideologists did claim to prove that the adulation of a Leader was strictly consistent with orthodox Marxist doctrine.[15]) Although Stalin made great efforts in private to ensure that his inordinate vanity and appetite for praise should be satisfied in public, his official style was always that of the modest servant and spokesman of 'the party'. To talk about anything other than 'collective' leadership of the party was 'stupid' he told the Congress described above after Kamenev's phrase had galvanized it into 'spontaneous' pandemonium. How could the party be led without Rykov, without Molotov, without Kalinin, without Tomskii, without Bukharin? By the time the speech was reprinted in Stalin's collected works the names of three, who had in the meantime been liquidated, had to be omitted. Like Hitler, Stalin knew that a lie to be effective had to be big. So, it was perhaps not surprising that the façade of state and legal machinery, created in embryo by Lenin, was only perfected by Stalin. The Soviets created by Lenin were from very early on dominated by the party, and elections to them were rigged. The Soviets and other institutions and guarantees brought into being by the Stalin Constitution of 1936 were inaugurated at the very height of the purges of 1936–38, and it was presumably never intended by Stalin that they should be more than a façade to deceive the credulous foreigner, and perhaps some idealistic theorists still remaining alive inside the Soviet Communist Party. The state and the law certainly never offered any threat of potential rivalry to Stalin's power as Leader. But, as will be seen, the case was different so far as the party was concerned, until the time when he had fully subjugated it after 1936. The party, after all, had revolutionary tradition and ideological legitimacy behind it, while the state had not.

It will be necessary to return to the discussion of further aspects of the nature of this Leadership system of domination which characterized the three prototype régimes. For the moment it is important to note at the outset that the three Leaders, whatever they may have said or whatever the theory in accordance with which they operated may have had to say about it, were concerned to establish each his own, personal rule, and not that of the party as an institution, and equally not that of the state machine as an established legal entity.

The subjugation of the legal order

In the context of the European tradition, with which alone we are for the moment concerned, the notion of law and legal order as being the foundations upon which all legitimate state authority rests is of very long standing. It was a virtually unbroken medieval conception that the king is under the law: the conception that the king is above the law—the doctrine of absolutism—'was an innovation' of which there was little trace 'in the Middle Ages, except insofar as it can be found among some of the Civilians'.[16] Even at the height of absolutism, the emancipation from the law claimed or conceded by the monarch was not entirely without practical limits; and in any case the 'barbarous innovation' of absolutism (as the leading historians of medieval political thought describe it) was overtaken almost everywhere in Europe by the movement towards the notion of monarchy limited by law, to which the monarch himself is subject. Some of the eighteenth-century philosophers of freedom even perceived that the danger to freedom was not necessarily, or so much, the crude absolute ruler, but the benevolent absolute ruler. Kant wrote in 1793 with considerable prophetic vision:

> A government might be established on the principle of benevolence towards the people, like that of a father towards his children. Under such a *paternal government* [*imperium paternale*] the subjects, as immature children who cannot distinguish what is truly useful or harmful to themselves, would be obliged to behave purely passively and to rely upon the judgment of the head of the state as to how they *ought* to be happy, and upon his kindness in willing their happiness at all. Such a government is the greatest conceivable *despotism*, i.e. a constitution which suspends the

entire freedom of its subjects, who henceforth have no rights whatever.[17]

The same thought can be found in Diderot. The danger that the mass of men would be taken in by tempting promises or hopes held out by absolutist rulers and thus forfeit the legal rights on which alone their freedom as individuals depended is one which can be discerned as a constantly recurrent theme in the history of Western political thought.

The only safeguard against the would-be benevolent despot lies in legal order. This means much more than the existence of laws enacted in accordance with the particular forms which are laid down at any particular time: in Germany Hitler had only to say 'off with his head', and not only would the order be carried out, but learned lawyers would write volumes or articles explaining that the real essence of German law was to be found in the will of the Führer. The way for this prostitution of their interests in the service of expediency by some (not all) German lawyers may perhaps have been paved by the course of German legal theory. The dominant legal theory in the late nineteenth century and in the twentieth century was positivism. The main exponent of this theory was Georg Jellinek, whose lectures at Heidelberg and *Allgemeine Rechtslehre*, first published in 1900, educated generations of lawyers and judges. The state, in Jellinek's doctrine, is the sole source of legal authority—though the validation of the law depends on the acknowledgement by the nation of the legitimate authority of the state. The only limits on the power of the state are those which it voluntarily submits to—this is the foundation of the traditional German *Rechtsstaat*, or state based on law. Jellinek, however, did also concede that there were certain moral and traditional limits on state action, but even these slender limits of state power were swept aside in the so-called 'Pure Theory of Law' propounded after 1911 by Hans Kelsen, which exercised great influence on the generation of lawyers who were active in the Weimar Republic. For Kelsen law is a norm enforced by the power of the state and nothing more: its moral or other content, its purpose, its acceptance are all matters with which the lawyer has no concern.

Where there is a state there is a legal order: and the legal order is the state in action. State and law are therefore one; and it follows that every state is necessarily a *Rechtsstaat*.[18]

Clearly, if law is viewed from this positivist standpoint and legitimacy is thus irrelevant as a component of state authority, then law could not be expected to be much of a safeguard against any actual exercise of power by the Leaders with whom we are concerned. In fact neither Hitler nor Stalin found that law was much of an obstacle to his plans in view of the ease with which each of them could enact new laws or amend existing laws at will, in the full certainty that the new or amended laws would be carried into effect. But while individual laws as such are no obstacle, the legal *order* can well become one—in other words, the persistence of an established system of rules, habits, and institutions operating within a fixed framework of limits, each single component part of which has to be overcome or set aside by a special enactment. And even if the old enactments can easily be replaced by new enactments, so long as the 'legal order' ensures that all existing enactments are complied with until repealed or amended, they necessarily present some barrier to free, unconstrained, arbitrary action by the Leader, if only by creating delay. Hitler and his leading henchmen frequently complained about the persistence of such legal order in Germany —Hitler indeed, like Marx and Lenin, had an overwhelming contempt for lawyers.

An interesting example from Germany of the intrusion of the legal order into the freedom of action which the Leader demands was provided by the history of the mass murder of the Jews.

> Although the historical evidence is not conclusive, it would seem that ... the Nüremburg Laws were calculated to bring to an end the previous legal uncertainty which had provided a fruitful field for terrorism of all descriptions; at least the laws produced a norm giving the victims certain possibilities of protecting themselves. The factual content of the racial laws was of course evil; in comparison to the previously existing situation, however, it was at least measurable evil, and all experience of existence under totalitarian

tyranny shows that this is more tolerable than sheer unpredictable arbitrary action. . . . Persecution of the Jews with complete social ostracism and ultimate genocide as its aim, was, of course, general National Socialist policy, and so the breathing space gained by the Nüremburg Laws was short-lived. Illegal measures became the rule once more, and finally culminated in mass murder. The murderers could not, however, quote the Nüremburg Laws as even partial legal justification for their actions: these Laws were not a link in the chain of non-official terrorism; instead they formed a temporary break in it.[19]

At the root of the Führer's authority lay 'Hitler's claim to an overriding power accorded to him by history. . . .' Accordingly the will of the Führer was binding primarily on 'ideological' grounds; it was *legally* binding only in so far as the Führer might from time to time decide to set a norm or when his instructions happened to coincide 'with existing laws, or the existing legal order'. No court could pronounce on the validity of the Führer's will: only History.[20]

It was precisely in order to get around the legal order that words such as 'History', 'Higher Law', or 'Supreme Interest of the Party', and the like were so frequently resorted to by the Leaders in order to justify their most outrageous acts. Mussolini, as might be expected, did less violence to the legal order than Hitler. Even so, it was unavoidable that his assumption in January 1925 of supreme power by what was essentially a revolutionary act should lead to some attempts to interfere with the traditional legal order. These attempts did not, in comparison with German experience, amount to very much. Some ideological additions were made in the sphere of offences against the state in the new Penal Code in 1931, and new and heavier penalties, including the death penalty, introduced; there were attempts to interfere with the traditional rights of the accused, to the accompaniment of ideological bombast by the legal apologists of Fascism in such terms as the overriding right of the totalitarian state to disregard mere individual rights, or ignore the maxim *nullum crimen sine lege* when the higher justice of the state interest demanded it. Magistrates and judges were harangued with

Fascist incantations: with some exceptions, they mostly remained fairly independent. There were repeatedly individual cases of injustice under Mussolini: but there was no successful and complete subjugation of the legal order in practice, only the loud expression of intention to do so.[21]

Stalin faced a much simpler problem because so far as legal order was concerned there was virtually none there to subjugate. The reform of the Russian legal system of 1864 had left the country with a bench and a bar of the highest standards—when they were permitted to function freely without interference from the powerful executive, which retained much of its arbitrary power even in the semi-constitutional period after 1906. The Bolsheviks on their advent to power swept law, bench and bar away. New civil and criminal codes and a system of courts emerged in the period of the New Economic Policy after 1921. But there were at least three reasons why the new Soviet 'legal order' never took root, or indeed really existed.

In the first place the codes themselves reflected the 'higher law of the Revolution' in the virtually unlimited discretionary powers which were conferred upon the courts, usually presided over by lay Communists, in all cases of 'socially dangerous' acts. Secondly, side by side with the courts, the growing security service wielded powers which were not only very wide, but which were often governed by secret instructions; and its actions could not be challenged in the courts. And thirdly, the exponents of legal theory for the most part accepted orthodox Marxist doctrine that the law was soon destined to 'wither away' along with the state, and to be replaced by a system of simple administration (whatever this notion may mean). Stalin, along with his Constitution, created a new system of courts, enacted ostensible guarantees of civil rights and judicial independence, and sternly put down all ideological speculation about the withering away of the state. At the same time he ensured that no means were available to protect the guaranteed civil rights in the courts, that judicial independence could always be overriden by party policy, and that the powers of the security service were substantially increased. Whatever problems Stalin faced in the preservation of his supreme power, legal order was never one of them.

While both Hitler and Stalin treated law with cynical indifference, there was a difference of style between the two men which, perhaps reflected the different traditions in which each operated—the tradition of the *Rechtsstaat* in Germany, and the Marxist indifference to law in the Soviet Union. Himmler told the German Law Academy (on October 11, 1936) how, when the National Socialists took over the police, they did so 'on the assumption that it did not matter in the least if our actions were contrary to some paragraph in the law. . . . There was, of course, talk abroad . . . of the police and therefore the state being in a condition of lawlessness. They called it lawless because it did not correspond to their conception of law. In fact, by what we did we laid the foundations for a new code of law, the law of destiny of the German people.'[22] Stalin would never have said that: on the contrary, it was precisely at the very climax of wholesale disregard for all existing legal rules, in 1936, that Stalin devoted particular attention, with his foreign admirers in mind, to creating a façade of strict, socialist legality. Each form of tyranny was effective in its own time and place.

Control over private morality

'We recognize nothing private,' Lenin maintained. 'Our morality,' he told young Communists in 1920, 'is entirely subordinated to the interests of the class struggle of the proletariat. . . . We do not believe in eternal morality.'[23] Since the class struggle of the proletariat was, in accordance with Lenin's belief directed by the Communist Party, it followed that moral questions could not be left to the individual, but were the concern of the guiding force of society, the party. This was indeed a logical position to adopt for any revolutionary Leader whose aim was no less than the complete transformation of both society and man. The sphere of private morality is closely linked to legal order. The aim of legal order, in the European tradition, is to safeguard by a system of enforced rules that minimum sphere within which the liberty of all is protected from the license of some. Outside this minimum sphere the law does not, or should not, seek to enforce moral duties or moral beliefs: 'the achievements of self-discipline . . . must in any theory of morality be a constituent of a good life. But what is valuable here is *voluntary* restraint, not submission to coercion. . . .'[24] It is, of course, the case that such a view has not always prevailed in European experience. The struggle of Church and state, Spain under Philip II, Geneva in the time of Calvin, all spring to mind, and it is indeed sometimes argued that some kind of parallel to 'totalitarianism' is to be sought in the theocratic societies of the past.[25] The liberal doctrine of the separation of church and state is above all designed to provide institutional protection against such 'totalitarian' trends.

The overwhelming importance attached in the Fascist and Communist states to ideology and to the leading rôle of the party naturally had the effect of undermining the whole concept of private, individual moral judgement. Fascist, National Socialist, and Soviet ideology alike asserted that the individual finds real fulfilment only in identification with the state, or with the party. The philosopher of Fascism, Giovanni Gentile, explained the Fascist theory of the individual in the following terms: 'And so, nothing private; and no limits to state action.' Totalitarianism, he continues,

> . . . appears to make the state swallow the individual, and to absorb into authority completely the liberty that should be set against every authority that limits it. . . . But one might say just the opposite: for in this conception the state is the will of the individual himself in its universal and absolute aspect, and thus the individual swallows the state, and since legitimate authority cannot extend beyond the actual will of the individual, authority is resolved completely in liberty. Lo and behold, absolutism is overturned and appears to have changed into its opposite, and the true absolute democracy is not that which seeks a limited state but that which sets no limit to the state that develops in the inmost heart of the individual, conferring on his will the absolutely universal force of law.[26]

It follows from such a view of the individual which (pseudo-Hegelian dialectics apart), is very close both to the National Socialist and the Soviet views, that there can be no room for the private moral judgement which sets itself up against the form of public morality imposed by the state or the party. As, indeed, Gentile had said as far back as 1925, 'it is impossible to be fascists in politics and non-fascists . . . in schools, non-fascists in our families, non-fascists in our daily occupations. . . .'[27]: the claims of both the National Socialists and the Soviet Communists under Stalin were in no way different.

But claims are one thing, fulfilment is another. The ruling powers can do a number of things. They can prohibit all utterances of which they disapprove: this is the oldest form of tyrannical or even merely autocratic rule, a strict censorship. They can go further and insist, as certainly Stalin insisted, that people should not remain silent, but should actually say or write the required things in the approved form. Thirdly, they can, by control over education and over all information entering the country, and by the extensive use of modern technical methods of propaganda, and monopoly of propaganda, indoctrinate or condition the inhabitants in such a way that they voluntarily believe what the ruling élite requires them to believe. Indeed, it is the desire to make an assault on the individual's private moral judgement which lies behind the monopoly over the means of information and communication which each of the three régimes under discussion endeavoured to assert. Nevertheless, the experience of over fifty years suggests that none of these methods singly, nor the sum total of them all, has been able completely to dominate the human mind or to eliminate private moral judgement, even if it remains unuttered, or remains unuttered for a very long time. The survival of resistance inside National Socialist Germany, in spite of the terrifying risk involved, was one proof of this.[28] The short-lived experience in Hungary in 1956 and in Czechoslovakia in 1968 was another. The growth of the dissent movement inside the Soviet Union in the course of the 1960s is a third.

It is small cause for wonder that, of the three régimes, that of Mussolini was by far the least successful in achieving the kind of complete control over private individual morality that Gentile had postulated as the essence of Fascism. For one thing Mussolini never resorted to the same extent to the organized terror and brutality of which Hitler and Stalin were masters; nor did his embryonic security force approximate to those which arose in Germany and in Soviet Russia. Secondly, Mussolini never succeeded in neutralizing or subduing the Church: the Church remained a formidable guardian of the private conscience, in a country where Catholicism was an influential force (to say nothing of the physical presence of the Vatican in Rome), in spite of some prudent compromises with the Fascist régime. In concluding the Concordat with the Vatican in 1931 'Fascism looked to make . . . and in large measure succeeded in making—use of the Catholic Church in order to bolster its own prestige and in order to strengthen both its internal and its external position. But in so doing it renounced in the most definite manner all hegemony over the spiritual formation of Italians and accepted a dangerous partition of spheres of influence with the Church.'[29] As Pope Pius XI explained in 1931, the state could only claim 'subjective totalitarianism', meaning by that 'that the totality of the citizen shall be obedient to and dependent on the State for all things which are within the competence of the State. . . .' But 'objective totalitarianism', which subordinates the citizen's whole life, 'individual, domestic, spiritual and supernatural' to the state was a 'manifest absurdity', and 'would be a monstrosity were its realization to be attempted in practice'.[30]

In Germany neither the Lutheran nor the Catholic Church was able to retain anything like the independence which the Roman Church asserted in Italy (whether because of Hitler's greater skill and ruthlessness or for other reasons is not in this context material).[31] In the case of the Soviet Union the chequered story of the rôle of the churches since 1917 cannot easily be summarized. Suffice it to say at this point that they have provided at different periods moral resistance in varying degrees to the encroachments of the party on the private sphere of the individual's conscience.[32]

The relation of church and state was a dominant issue in medieval Europe, and remained a constant problem in European politics thereafter. What are the proper limits of state power in the matter of individual conscience? And what are the consequences for individual liberty if the balance of power between state and church is disturbed in this respect? These were the two questions which predominated before the advent of the so-called 'totalitarian' countries. Today, in discussing those régimes to which the term 'totalitarian' may still be applicable—if there are such—new questions are raised. To what extent does the survival of some degree of church independence in such countries as the Soviet Union, Poland or Yugoslavia succeed in nullifying the claim of Communist parties to override the private conscience of the citizens, at any rate in all matters in which the policy of the party is involved? And secondly, what is the effect of such survival on the totality of power which the ruling élite claims in such countries, and indeed on the problem of whether 'totality' of power can ever have a meaning in practice? To some of these questions it will be necessary to return at the end of this enquiry.

Mobilization and mass legitimacy

The remaining two contours can be dealt with much more briefly. It is indeed evident that intensive and unremitting mobilization of the entire population characterized all three prototype régimes—primarily for war, in the cases of both Mussolini and Hitler, for the construction of Communism in Stalin's case. Harrying of the population as a means of preserving personal power has been the favourite device of tyrannous rulers since antiquity: Aristotle, after listing a number of very modern-sounding devices as characteristics of a tyrant, refers to the devices of warmongering, and of impoverishing his subjects so as to keep them so busy earning a pittance that they have no time left to plot.[33] No doubt the inspiration for the 'mobilization' of their populations, for Mussolini, Hitler and Stalin, derived from a variety of causes, ideological and psychological: this does not alter the fact that nothing provides a more convincing justification for terror than the claim, constantly reiterated, that the nation is pursuing some great and noble aim, to which all effort must be constantly devoted and that this aim is being frustrated by internal and external enemies who must be destroyed. Each Leader, in his own way, made full and constant use of this type of claim.

There are those who take the view that mobilization is the feature which primarily distinguishes the 'totalitarian' régime from a merely 'authoritarian' one.[34] (The term 'authoritarian' is open to some theoretical objections, since every legitimate government exercises 'authority'. But 'authoritarian' seems well established both in English and in American usage to designate a state in which obedience to authority is favoured as against liberty; and in which there is little control over the way in which authority is exercised.) It is true there are many cases of autocratic or police states where the rulers are quite content to leave things as they are, provided their own power is not endangered: they enforce disciplined obedience, but they have no ideological, revolutionary or warlike aims for the future so long as they can stay in the saddle. Spain under Franco is probably an example of such a polity, and thus differs in decisive respects from our three prototypes. Important as it is, however, it is doubtful if mobilization can thus be elevated to the rank of being the main distinguishing contour. Mobilization of the civilian population in time of war, for example, does not of itself produce a 'totalitarian' régime—as the examples of Britain and the United States in the Second World War showed. Or, to take an example from the ancient world, Julius Caesar certainly tried to effect enormous changes in Rome by what would now be described as mobilization; yet his rule fell in many respects short of what in our time has been described as 'totalitarian'. Other examples, ancient and modern, will have to be examined when the question of the novelty and uniqueness of 'totalitarianism' comes to be considered.

Nonetheless, the importance of this contour for giving the 'totalitarian' régimes their character cannot be underestimated, if only because of the excuse that mobilization provides for terror. An important aspect of total mobilization is that it logically entails the ultimate complete control over private property. And since property is one of the main safeguards of the individual against the encroachments of government, mobilization thereby contributes to total enslavement of the population. In the case of the Soviet Union, the abolition of private property was one of the aims of the Bolshevik revolution, but it was only effectively accomplished by Stalin after he had put an end to the New Economic Policy. In Italy and Germany where the contribution of the industrialists to the rise of Fascism and National Socialism was a major factor,

abolition of private property was not officially part of the pro-
gramme, and in Italy never took place: it is possible that the putting
into practice of the Corporative State would have made serious
inroads on private property rights, as well as on labour rights, but
the Corporative State remained largely a dead letter. National
Socialism contented itself, until the war, at any rate, with concerted
attacks on labour and on the property of Jews. The 'Aryan' industrialists who had helped Hitler to power certainly profited substantially from this aspect of National Socialist policy and from the
preparations for war. (It is of significance, however, that profit did
not mean power: as a recent investigation of the sources has shown,
the industrialists had no 'important formative influence on the
history of the "Third Reich" '.)[35] Moreover, by 1942 the National
Socialist régime had asserted a very complete degree of mobilization over all industry;[36] and one may well speculate whether, if
Hitler's régime had survived, the industrialists would have re-
covered their former relative freedom.

Even more important for the Leader and his ruling élite than
control over property was the consequential control which, in the
last resort, in all three régimes, they could assert over the livelihood
of every single individual. The assault on private property in the
Communist example, of course, made this particularly easy, since
the central authority became thereby the sole employer of all
labour; and the absence of private property denies this means of
defence to the individual who tries to emancipate himself by creating material independence. In Germany and Italy, and particularly
in the latter, the process of control did not go so far: though even
in these countries the demands of war led to very extensive control
over all economic resources; and, apart from war, the residual
power to interfere with property in an arbitrary manner was always
there. The control over individual employment is, however, by no
means confined to those areas where the enterprise or undertaking
is publicly controlled. This is because the Leader and his ruling
élite can by the exercise of their arbitrary power ensure the dismissal from his employment of virtually any individual or category
of individuals and, moreover, ensure that when once anyone has been
dismissed, it will not be possible for him to obtain employment

elsewhere except perhaps in a low menial capacity. When the question of terror in the 'totalitarian' polity is considered it becomes apparent that control over employment can, in practice, become an effective substitute for physical terror. The Soviet authorities today, for example, enforce conformity on intellectuals by dismissal or threat of dismissal from white-collar employment, with loss of its concomitant privileges, as often as by direct violent methods against the individuals concerned.

Finally, it is notable that all three prototype régimes claimed to derive their legitimacy from the mass of the people: in that sense they were a part of the democratic tradition which was born in the American and French revolutions rather than a part of the abso-lutist or autocratic tradition of the past. There is little need to stress this fact in the case of Communism. It is not only a matter of doctrine or ideology—of the fact that Marxism is a doctrine of liberation of mankind from its exploiters. In practice, Lenin and Stalin repeatedly laid stress on the democratic basis of the new order. Indeed, the Stalin Constitution of 1936 was, among other things, designed to reaffirm the close union between the people and their rulers on which the Soviet régime had always claimed to rest. The draft of the Constitution was submitted to mass discussion and to an approval of plebiscite: the fact that the party controlled both and that neither was genuine in the sense of being the spon-taneous or rational expression of approval is of no immediate significance. What we are concerned with here is the *symbol* of legitimacy, and there can be no doubt that this was and remains in the Soviet case mass democracy. Soviet elections play the same symbolic rôle. They cannot, in the nature of things, represent a genuine choice by the voter, since no choice of candidates is ever offered and all elections take place under the close eye of the party representative, and are so organized that the voter who wishes to do anything other than place the printed slip in the ballot box (such as write in an alternative name), has to draw attention to himself in front of a party or police observer. But a Soviet election symbolizes the mass legitimation of the régime; and, within Lenin's concep-tion of leadership by an élite over a mass that cannot be trusted spontaneously to do what is supposed to be good for it, represents an act of mass democracy.

In spite of the fact that Fascism and National Socialism derived from quite a different political tradition, the mass democratic legitimation by the Leaders of their régime was constantly evident. The rigged plebiscites and elections were considered as much a necessity as under Communism. Besides, who could doubt that both Mussolini and Hitler were masters at moulding the emotions of vast crowds to give the appearance of popular support to their actions? As Mussolini told Emil Ludwig, 'the capacity of the modern man for faith is illimitable. When the masses are like wax in my hands, when I stir their faith . . . I feel myself to be a part of them. All the same there persists in me a certain feeling of aversion, like that which the modeller feels for the clay he is moulding.' He went on to say that a dictator could be loved as well, 'provided that the masses fear him at the same time. The crowd loves strong men. The crowd is like a woman.'[37]

For all the insistence of Fascist doctrine on obedience, leadership, hierarchy and the like, official ideology nonetheless went through all kinds of contortions in order to prove that the 'totalitarian state' was really the most perfect form of democracy. Some of Gentile's utterances on this question have already been quoted. In Hitler's case the importance played by the race, the *Volk*, in National Socialist ideology, of itself created a base for mass democratic legitimacy. Carl Schmitt, the official ideologist of National Socialism, argued that the history of the state in Europe was divided into three stages. The first was absolutism—the representative stage. The absolute monarch's service had been to reduce feudal anarchy to order: he 'represents' political unity. The French Revolution produced a counter-movement, which for a time combined two trends, liberalism and democracy, the false and the true. Liberalism corresponds to a *neutral* state (as under the Weimar Constitution in Germany): the aim of liberalism is to emancipate bourgeois society from the state altogether, and to destroy the logical, historically determined (*konsequent*) political form which grows out of absolutism, namely the third stage in history—the total *identity* state. In this state the *Volk* forms a unity 'through its effective homogeneity and its consciousness of its own political capacities [*Handlungsfähigkeit*]'. Popular sovereignty is at last made real in the strict and true sense.[38] Ideology apart, ostensible concern for the people, for the little man, attacks on 'plutocracy' and the like were an important part of National *Socialist* propaganda. In short, 'mass democracy' is one of the five clear contours which emerge from an examination of the three prototype 'totalitarian' régimes.

3/The Pillars of Totalitarianism

Why pillars?

Assuming that the analysis of the nature of leadership in the three prototype régimes as outlined in the last chapter is correct, then it follows that to speak of 'institutions' in a totalitarian society could be misleading. An institution is a complex of legal and conventional relationships and practices. An institution operates within a political system as an independent element, with a certain measure of political life of its own. Its sphere of action may be limited, its capacity restricted: but its actions are its own, or substantially its own. It may be influenced by, or constrained by, many factors: but within the limits of its freedom of action it is independent. For example, the Duma in Russia after 1906 was an institution in this sense; but a Soviet is not. The Duma was hampered and restricted in its actions, it could be dissolved by the emperor at will, its sphere of competence was limited, it was subject to executive interference—it was nonetheless a free agent because its actions, while it acted, were its own: the fact alone of the constant struggle which was waged against it by the executive power showed that it was free. A Soviet in contrast is a façade for something else—normally the Communist Party. Its debates follow a predetermined pattern, its actions, even if they take the form of, and purport to be, deliberations and decisions, are in fact formal acts expressing neither decisions nor deliberations, but compliance with a previous decision taken elsewhere—usually in the appropriate organ of the Communist Party.

Now, of course, the Soviet is an extreme case of a façade of a mock institution, behind which some more real institution, like the party, operates. The party, the machinery of the state, and the whole apparatus built around the ideology and its enforcement, are perhaps much nearer to real institutions. Yet, even in their case, the Leader always seeks to dominate them, at any rate to the extent of preventing them from acquiring such independence of action as may threaten his own position, or his monopoly of power. Even if he has not always been successful (and indeed it may be the case that complete and lasting success in this respect is an impossibility), nevertheless, since the Leader's aim is always to frustrate their functioning as real institutions it seems better to choose a different term to describe the three main instruments which the Leader uses to maintain himself in power. Hence, the neutral term 'pillar' has been selected. For, just as the five 'contours' disclosed the general character of the totalitarian régime, so there appear to be in each of the countries under examination three distinctive 'pillars' upon which the Leader's rule is based. These are, first, a so-called ideology, with all the means which may be considered both for enforcing compliance with it and for excluding rival ideologies; secondly, a party which has grown out of a more informal movement; and thirdly the administrative machinery of the state, which in the totalitarian régime displays quite distinctive characteristics. There are, of course, other instruments available to the Leader— the army, or the police, for example. But, apart from the fact that they are the ones which are most closely controlled by the Leader and by the ruling élite, they are less distinctive than the three 'pillars' selected for discussion.

Ideology

'Ideology' is one of the most disputed terms in the language of politics. In its origins it meant the science of ideas. As used nowadays it frequently denotes a system of beliefs which relate to fundamental political aims and, moreover, a system which is designed, consciously or unconsciously, to influence and direct the course of action of those who are within its sphere of influence. In this general sense 'ideology' can be applied to a wide variety of systems of belief. It would include something as comprehensive as the official Soviet ideology, 'Marxism-Leninism', as well as, say, the basic tenets of the British Labour Party. It can even be used to describe the beliefs which a nation, consciously or unconsciously, inculcates in its citizens by a whole variety of means. It may stand for some peculiar national value or habit which is neither consistent, nor logical] Thus, to take an example once used by Pareto, faith in 'equality' in the United States prevents one from getting one's shoes polished in some hotels, because it is contrary to 'equality' for one man to polish another's shoes. Yet 'equality' in American usage does not extend to the Negro or the Japanese inhabitants in most elementary matters. (Pareto was, of course, writing in 1912.) Here, 'ideology', in the broad sense in which the word is frequently used, helps to obscure or make acceptable something that would be absurd if regarded rationally.[1]

But since we are concerned with ideology in the three totalitarian societies, it is necessary to look at the sense which Marx gave to the term, and which in turn influenced Lenin—and through Lenin, influenced Stalin, and directly or indirectly, Mussolini and Hitler. It is no exaggeration to say that Marx's views on ideology dominate political discussion of the subject. Now for Marx ideology is closely linked to a social class: the content of the ideology is determined by the production relations which obtain in a particular society. It is illusory in Marx's view to suppose that ideas exist, as it were, in the abstract, exercising some kind of force of their own on human action. On the contrary, they reflect the material interests of the ruling class—that is to say, in a modern society of Marx's day, of the bourgeoisie. This 'ideology' of the bourgeoisie cannot be changed by other ideas: it can only be changed by the coming to power of another class, of the proletariat, which by seizing power abolishes classes and class rule forever. The proletariat has no ideology since it is not at present the ruling class: and when it abolishes classes by coming to power, there will no longer be need for ideology.[2]

It was from Marx, therefore, that 'ideology' originally derived its somewhat tarnished image as a deceptive (or self-deceptive), or even hypocritical set of ideas which really served self-interest, while purporting to express ideals. But wide currency to this view of ideology was also given by Pareto. For Pareto all ideologies are equally suspect—unlike Marx, he makes no exception for the proletariat. But ideologies are important because they 'transcend cold realities', they are based on 'derivations' which are rationalized, deeply rooted human urges. When the engineer has found the best machine, Pareto argues, he can sell it on the basis of a logical argument. But social measures can only be promoted by sentiment, and 'especially if the sentiment is heightened and takes on a religious form. It is all the better if it expresses itself in enthusiastic derivations, soaring above cold realities. . . .' In this respect Pareto acknowledges his debt to Georges Sorel for whom the strength of a social doctrine lies not in its truth (indeed Sorel suggests at times that truth may be a weakness in promoting a social doctrine) but in the fact that it becomes a driving force through being accepted as a myth.[3] Even a cursory view of the three prototype régimes is sufficient to make it plain that the ideologies upon which they were based derived their great strength less from the truth of what they proclaimed or promised than from the deep, instinctive response which they evoked in the mass of the population, or from the myths which they engendered in people's minds.

So, for Marx ideology is in effect a fraud by the bourgeoisie, which only the victory of the proletariat—which has no need of ideology or any other fraud—can put an end to. For Pareto all ideologies, by whomsoever held, partake of the fraudulent: but that is their intrinsic nature, and they are none the worse or less necessary for that. An entirely new dimension to the understanding of ideology was added by Lenin in his main theoretical work on revolution, *What Is To Be Done?*, published in 1902. Unlike both Marx and Pareto, for whom ideology seems to be something which is spontaneously, almost unconsciously, generated, Lenin was concerned with the way in which an ideology arises. There are only two possible kinds of ideology, he says—bourgeois and socialist— since all ideology is the product of class interests. This is already very different from the view of Marx, because for Marx the proletariat, which comes to power in order to abolish class rule, requires no ideology: in the words of the *Communist Manifesto*, the theory of the Communists 'may be summed up in the single sentence: Abolition of private property.' Lenin's revolutionary class certainly requires a 'socialist' ideology: but he goes much further than that. This socialist ideology, he says, will never develop of its own accord: on the contrary, if left to its own spontaneous development, the working class movement will inevitably become subordinated to the bourgeois ideology. The reason for this inevitable process is that bourgeois ideology is much older in origin, and much more developed than socialist ideology, and 'disposes of *immeasurably* more effective means for spreading itself'. The only remedy for this state of affairs lies in leadership: the intellectual élite must lead the workers and must bring socialist ideology into their movement 'from the outside'. The whole notion that an ideology has to be, as it were, artificially injected into a class, and then cultivated, nurtured, and protected, appears for the first time in Lenin.[4] Since, as will be seen, the strength of the ideology in each of the three prototype societies lay much less in its content than in the manipulative political devices with which it was engendered, fostered and protected, this addition by Lenin to Marx (and Pareto) acquires outstanding importance for the present enquiry.

Not of course that the content of the ideologies with which we are now concerned was immaterial to their success: however much the Leader is prepared to rely on force and fraud in order to achieve, and to keep himself in, power, it is plain that the more persuasive the qualities of the ideology of his movement are, the easier it will be for him to govern. Therefore, an ideology must appeal to the deep instincts of the mass of the people, to their traditions, their emotions, their hatreds, fears and hopes. The reactions to the three ideologies were very similar—for example, the mass hysteria and the surrender to the Leader's will; all shared one feature in common—the enemy (the Jew, the capitalist, the imperialists); all three appealed to nationalism, which is everywhere the predominant and most primitive mass emotion. Fascism and National Socialism were primarily nationalistic creeds from their inception; and it is notable that Marxism–Leninism, in the hands of Stalin, became in many significant respects more specifically nationalist in content than it had been under Lenin (Socialism in one country— the USSR: or 'proletarian internationalism', meaning 'Support Soviet might as the first priority'). Nonetheless, it is true to say that in all three systems it was the style of leadership which always predominated over any kind of doctrinal system.

For Mussolini doctrine came as an afterthought: it was the boast of Fascism before power was seized that it was a movement for action, and not a doctrine. As Mussolini himself emphasized, the theory or purpose behind action was largely irrelevant; it was the battle that mattered. And indeed, the strength of Fascism lay in the violence of its opposition to whatever was the enemy of the moment, and in the emotional content of its slogans. When the time came to put Fascism into the form of a doctrine, in an article for the *Enciclopedia Italiana* signed by Mussolini but in part composed by Gentile,[5] the vapidity of the phrases revealed the intellectual poverty behind the movement.

> We represent a new principle in the world, the clear, final and categorical antithesis of democracy, plutocracy, Freemasonry and the immortal principles of 1789. . . . The ideals of democracy are exploded, beginning with that of 'progress'. Ours is an aristocratic country; the state of all will end by becoming the state of a few. . . . The Fascist conception of the state is all-embracing, and outside of the state no human or spiritual values can exist, let alone be desirable.

And so on. It is not surprising that many competent critics regard castor oil and the 'cosh' as the only original contributions which Fascism made to political thought.[6] Much of Gentile's attempts to turn Fascism into a political doctrine reads like sad nonsense. Actually, Gentile was regarded by Mussolini with some suspicion (as an intellectual) and on a number of occasions repudiated.[7] It was Gentile, however, who with some justice, writing in 1928, explained that Fascism was neither a philosophical system nor a religion, but rather a method of action. 'The "real" views of the *Duce* are those which he formulates and executes at one and the same time,'[8] he wrote in terms recalling the Marxist's unity of theory and practice. To the end, Fascism remained a posturing, a part played out in public by the Leader, without reality, without an intellectual framework, without consistency and without serious intellectual (as distinct from political) posterity. The impetus which drove Mussolini to power was in large measure shame at Italy's discomfiture in the First World War, and the desire to wipe out that shame by military conquests. And so he drove a people which did not desire it to war and defeat. His posturing flattered their vanity. His failure alienated their support overnight.

If Fascism was a part enacted in public, National Socialism was necromancy: its reliance on symbolism, myth, mass hypnosis, and ritual was much the greater. With Marxism–Leninism the case is different, since there is no doubt that a serious intellectual framework lay behind the transformation of the doctrines of Marx which was effected by Lenin. We are however concerned with Stalin not with Lenin—it is the Russia of Stalin which is one of our three prototypes, not the Russia of Lenin. Now, so far as Stalin was concerned, his crude simplification of the doctrine which Lenin had propagated, and the additions which he made to it in the interests of the preservation of his own power would seem to justify the view that in his case too the content of the ideology was subordinated to its utility as an instrument of rule. To choose one example only. In connection with the New Economic Policy, launched in 1921, Lenin had repeatedly emphasized the need for a long period of 'class peace', of reconciliation between town and country. This was a serious and responsible, if somewhat naïve, recognition by Lenin that a socialist revolution had been made prematurely in Russia, before social conditions existed which could justify it, and that nothing but a long period of social harmony could allow socialism to develop by voluntary effort. All this was reversed by Stalin who, for reasons unconnected with doctrine, decided to plunge the country into the fever of the successive purges of 1936–38. But doctrine was duly amended to suit policy and the exacerbation of the class struggle during the period of the construction of socialism put forward as a part of Marxist orthodoxy. Such examples could be multiplied.

This, therefore, is one respect in which the manipulated ideology[9] of the 'totalitarian' Leaders differed from the 'false consciousness' of the bourgeoisie, in Marx's (or rather Engels's) terminology, or the 'derivation' of the ruling élite, in the language of Pareto. Another is the way in which the Leader can and does enforce a monopoly for his ideology. This is one of the purposes for which he requires control over all the means of public communication—press and broadcasting in particular, though censorship on the import of books and some means of control over the universities and other seats of instruction may be equally important. By such means he can do much more than propagate his own chosen ideology: he can make sure that no rival ideas or doctrines, or any criticism of his own, ever reaches the minds of the people over whom he rules, except in the garbled form which is considered by the propaganda experts to be no longer dangerous. Of course, the complete enforcement of such a monopoly is far from easy. Mussolini failed completely, if only to the extent that the rival ideology of the Church was readily available. Stalin certainly achieved the highest degree of success in this respect, though even in his case it was probably only a relative success.

Closely connected, but not identical with, monopoly is the fact that the Leader is able to propagate his chosen ideology in, as it were, a vacuum of information. To enforce a monopoly for an ideology is to keep out rival systems which could displace the official ideology. To enforce a vacuum means much more: it means keeping out both arguments and factual information which could in any way challenge the official ideology. Thus, even some of the basic thought of Marx has been suppressed at different periods in the Soviet Union. The most notable example of this is the suppression by Stalin of Marx's analysis of the 'Asiatic mode' of production, which, if pursued to its logical conclusion, in effect challenges any claim which the Soviet form of rule may have to be in any way related to Marx's theory of society. For the 'Asiatic mode' is distinguished by its stagnant social character, in which the ruling power virtually holds the bulk of the country in subjection, both as to its property and as to employment, in a state analogous to slavery. It is the antithesis of feudalism—the stage out of which modern capitalism, and thence socialism and Communism, according to Marx, inevitably evolve. Now if Russia in its pre-revolutionary stage belongs more properly to the 'Asiatic mode' than to feudalism—which Marx at one time believed and which is a convincingly arguable case—the whole Marxist or quasi-Marxist analysis of all that has happened since 1917 is put in jeopardy. Stalin, realizing this after a discussion on the 'Asiatic mode' of production had taken place (in muted terms) in Leningrad in 1931, virtually excised the 'Asiatic mode' from the canon of Marxism, so far as the Soviet public was concerned.[10] This is only one of many striking examples of the way in which the Leader can ensure that the ideas which he wishes to propagate are bred in a vacuum of his own making. Mussolini was never able to achieve this vacuum. Hitler, though much more successful, nevertheless fell far short of Stalin: Stalin's skill in this respect was an important factor in the consolidation of his power.

Control over information should, at best, from the Leader's point of view, take a number of forms. Negatively, it should be able to exclude all information and argument which may be inconsistent with the official ideology, or can throw doubt on it, let alone attempt to rival it. This can be very extensive: as experience under Stalin showed, the exclusion and control can reach the stage where virtually no subject is exempt from suspicion. The study of history is perhaps an obvious field in which seemingly innocent discussion of the past can carry implications critical of the present: the Soviet authorities have always been fully aware of this. But the implications of criticism or deviation from ideological purity were not always so readily apparent in some of the other spheres where in the period of Stalin's rule negative controls were applied: the circus, for example, or music. No doubt one has to reckon in such cases with an element of paranoia on the part of the Leader, or with the excessive zeal induced by panic among subordinate officials, fearful for their own safety if the Leader should once suspect that they are failing in their duty of spotting heresies.

Apart from negative exclusion, there is positive propagation. The Leader is not content merely that his ideology should not be challenged or laid open to doubt: he is actively concerned to ensure by all means available to him that it is believed, or at all events reiterated, by as many people as possible, and as often as possible. To use Lenin's phrase, he seeks to bring consciousness into the mass from without. And it is indeed to the mass that the Leader's main effort is directed: he woos, cajoles, bewitches, befuddles, and blinds the mass with all the instruments which his skill, his imagination, his resources, above all, his style, make possible. Mussolini in this sense was a showman: he acted out his part in front of a people

to Communist usage. In Communist usage 'propaganda' has no mass connotation, but on the contrary relates to the education of a small minority in order to convey to it the whole system of ideas which comprise the correct revolutionary theory or doctrine. Where it is a matter of indoctrinating a mass of many people with one, preferably simple, idea, the term used since the time of Plekhanov and Lenin has always been 'agitation'. The description current in the Soviet Union for the general activity of the Communist Party in all spheres of its educational activity is 'Agitation and Propaganda', abbreviated to 'Agitprop'.)

All means of communication with the population should, ideally, be in the Leader's control if he is to hope to be effective in the indoctrination which he pursues. Not only the obvious means such as press, radio, education and publishing should be controlled, but private written and verbal communication, as far as possible. The means of clandestine dissemination, such as the duplicating machine, should also be controlled: in Soviet law to this day such a machine is unobtainable without a license. However, it is not only a question of control: it is also a question of the technical means available to the Leader to subject people to his control. The importance of modern technological devices in the emergence of totalitarianism has repeatedly, and rightly, been stressed in the literature. The importance extends, of course, to weapons, to all means of surveillance and to rapidity of transport; but in the context of ideology it is wireless telegraphy and telephony which stand out as the most immediately important. No other instrument enables the Leader to penetrate right into the homes of even a large and widely dispersed population: no other instrument can with such ease and rapidity impose uniformity of standards and universality of judgement (though, needless to say, this aspect of broadcasting is by no means confined to the so-called totalitarian societies). It is only by the use of the radio that the Leader in the present century was first enabled to talk literally to the whole population in times of particular stress, and indeed at other times as well. At the time of Lenin's victory in 1917 radio broadcasting was still in its infancy. But by the time Stalin was on the ascent to power it had been fully developed.

Such then are the ways in which an ideology can be manipulated for the purposes of mass appeal and hence of mass control, in the sense of winning over mass support. Of course, the Leader pursues a variety of aims in launching and promoting his ideology—gratification of personal vanity was an obvious aim in the case of all the three Leaders with whom we are presently concerned. The subversion of liberty is another. As Adam Ferguson pointed out (before ideologies were known as such) an official ideology and freedom are incompatible. 'The love of the public and respect to its laws, are the points in which mankind are bound to agree; but if, in matters of controversy, the sense of any individual or party is invariably pursued, the cause of freedom is already betrayed.'[11] But there are three main aims which a manipulated ideology is designed to serve: legitimacy, anaesthesia, and mobilization.

The pursuit and strengthening of the legitimacy of its rule is probably the primary political function of every ideology. The bourgeoisie, in the eyes of Marx, uses its ideology in order to make its exploitation of the proletariat more acceptable; the ruling élite, according to Pareto, bolsters its rule by the 'derivations' which conceal, or render more palatable, the truth. The Leader of the totalitarian régime, however, has much greater need of asserting his legitimacy, and therefore all the greater need of his manipulated ideology for this purpose. Unlike the bourgeoisie, the Leader has come to recent power by a revolutionary act or movement: he has no tradition of rule, whether dynastic or elected. His revolutionary act, therefore, requires justification in the eyes of the mass to whom he directs his appeal. This is one of the functions of ideology—to glorify, justify, and exalt the revolution, under whatever name it may be known: the March on Rome and the October Revolution were both, to a large extent mythical, since there was no 'March', but a political démarche made to a distraught government; and no 'revolution', in the sense that there was no popular uprising in October 1917 (in contrast with what happened in February 1917), but a seizure of power by the Bolshevik Red Guards. And a mythical revolution requires all the more bolstering by the mechanism of ideology. Apart from the mythical event upon which the Leader bases his legitimacy, he is also in need of doctrine to bolster his authority. This is all the more necessary where there is no clearly visible and recognizable source of legitimate authority to which the Leader can appeal, such as an election recognized to be free, or a clear, traditionally accepted dynastic claim.

So far as Hitler was concerned his electoral support in March 1933, the last occasion on which anything even approximating to a free election was held, never exceeded 43.9 per cent of the national vote, in spite of the intimidation, pressure, and propaganda to which the electorate had been subjected. Moreover, until the proscription of the Communists, the National Socialists had only a bare majority in the Reichstag with the support of their Nationalist allies.[12] Stalin could claim no better title in terms of an election—in the only reasonably free election held under Bolshevik rule, the elections to the Constituent Assembly in 1917, the Bolsheviks had polled around 25 per cent of the national vote; and all subsequent elections were openly rigged, and were known to have been rigged. Nor could Stalin rely, to any extent, on the dynastic claim deriving from Lenin: it was generally known, in the upper echelons of the party at all events, that Lenin had repudiated Stalin as his successor in the last active months of his life. And so each man mobilized the ideology to bolster his legitimacy. Hitler was not interested in basing his power on the fact that he had become chancellor—this would have involved all the limitations implied by the whole system of the formal state, with its laws and regulations, against which Hitler and his henchmen conducted an incessant campaign throughout the duration of the National Socialist régime. For Hitler the rôle of Leader required plenary, unlimited and unrestricted authority. And so the ideology stressed traditional Germanic leadership, the claims of the Führer as Leader of the German *Volk* and the like—all claims to authority which were vague and imprecise, but which transcended the limits and restrictions of state and constitution. In contrast, Mussolini's ideology (as has been seen) always stressed the supremacy of the state, and it was as leader of the state and as occupant of a number of specific state offices that Mussolini claimed to rule. This fact in itself was, no doubt, a measure of Mussolini's relative weakness.

Stalin's position was quite different. The notion of a leader was alien to Marxism and it would have been well-nigh impossible for Stalin to make his own personal leadership central to the ideology —though it will be recalled some of his more ingenious ideologists did occasionally try to reconcile Marxism and the *Führerprinzip*. Stalin's ideology, like Lenin's, always stressed the primacy of the Communist Party, and its historic claim to authority over all life of state and society. Of course, within the party Stalin knew how to assert and preserve his own supremacy because he was the master of the apparatus and the supreme manipulator of appointments. Moreover—as will be seen below—Stalin's assertion of personal supremacy over the party in the Soviet Union had exactly the same effect of crippling the party as an independent institution as Hitler's strong methods had in Germany. Nevertheless, it was the supremacy of the party which the ideology laboured above all else to preserve from any kind of challenge: to this day, to challenge the leading rôle of the party is the most serious heresy in the Communist world—as the Czechoslovak Communists learned to their cost in 1968.

Even if it be true that the assertion of legitimacy is not a function of ideology which is confined to the totalitarian régimes, the inducement of moral anaesthesia by means of ideology would seem to be a novel feature, at any rate on the scale practised by Hitler and Stalin. This function of ideology may be described as neutralizing by ideological justifications the serious moral revulsion against the atrocities and brutalities perpetrated by the Leader. It is a powerful aspect of this type of ideological persuasion that it is used to direct the hatred and execration of the mass of the population not against individuals so much as against certain classes of persons— Jews, or the bourgeoisie, or priests, or, even more vaguely, 'saboteurs', 'traitors', or 'Trotskyists'. The advantage of this singling out of a class as the enemy is threefold. In the first place, the masses can be the more easily persuaded that the hardships from which they suffer are the direct fault of this or that class of evil persons, and they are thus deflected away from criticism of the Leader. Secondly, and this is particularly true where the class of enemies is vague, anyone whom the Leader wishes to eliminate can be brought under the heading of membership of the class.

And thirdly, the ideological justifications adduced by the Leader anaesthetize the moral revulsion and generate the crowd hysteria which is necessary in order to make more acceptable the kind of terror upon which all arbitrary government relies for its survival and endurance. The National Socialist experience provides another aspect of this use of ideology to induce acceptance of large-scale atrocity. This was the use by National Socialist leaders, notably Hitler and Himmler, of arguments based on racial superiority or on appeals to history (both equally spurious) in order to persuade the decent, kindly German (as they were prone to describe them) to commit the acts of violence against Jews and Bolsheviks from which his true nature allegedly revolted.

The third main function of ideology, and one which is also usually peculiar to the totalitarian régimes (at all events, in time of peace), is to act as the instrument of the mobilization which was singled out earlier as one of the contours. This function is too obvious to require much emphasis. Each of the three ideologies concerned devoted considerable time to underlining the need for effort, whether in peace, or in war, or in preparation for war, justifying the exhortation to effort by promise of future glory, or happiness, or greatness.

The party

All the three prototypes were characterized by the important rôle played in each of them by a party; and in many respects, for all their distinctive ideologies, the three parties displayed similar features. Each developed out of a revolutionary movement, under a dominant Leader, of which the aim was capture of power. Each successfully captured power with a semblance of constitutional right and legality, thereby becoming one of several political parties in power. Lenin and Mussolini both ruled in nominal coalitions,—Lenin for six months, Mussolini for over two years—before finally eliminating all other parties. Hitler's course was similar. With the emergence of the movement, now become the party, into the dominant rôle as the sole political party, the end of party rule is brought about. Just as in Marx's view the victory of the proletariat puts an end to classes, so the victory of the movement puts an end to political parties: for a single 'party' is a contradiction in terms, since a political 'party' can mean only a competing body, competing for a 'part' in power.

So far, therefore, the course of the victory of the three movements with which we are concerned is broadly parallel—with the qualification that, unlike the other two Leaders, Stalin inherited a party which he did not himself either create or lead to victory. It was not therefore surprising that he should have transformed it in many respects when he did take it over. Lenin's concept of the party as the élite which was to provide leadership for the working class movement, and thereby save it from the inevitable defeat at the hands of the bourgeoisie which it would suffer if it were left to its own spontaneous devices, was, according to the most generally accepted view, an innovation in Marxist theory. But it would seem that the rôle which in practice he envisaged and created for the party after victory had been achieved was a startling innovation in the history of political institutions. There have been dominant political parties in the past: but the Bolshevik Party during Lenin's lifetime in office was a good deal more than that. It was designed to form, and to a large extent did form, the real power behind the elaborate façade of government organs which the new rulers erected in place of those that the revolution had destroyed: Soviets, trade unions, courts, commissariats, even in some respects the units and formations of the army. The Bolshevik Party was equipped with its own organs of repression and with its own special forces. In so far as the 'façade' machinery—especially the Soviets and the trade unions—attempted to assert some independence against the party, Lenin struggled against them, and by 1921 had defeated them. In the process the party became more centralized and more disciplined; and the remnants of rival parties which had still managed to survive were finally eliminated from the scene.[13]

But though Lenin dominated and disciplined the party, and exacted submission in return for the monopolistic rôle which it was enabled to enjoy in society, the Communist Party during his active lifetime did not cease to function as an institution with some degree of life and independence of its own. Until 1921, at any rate, free dissent was tolerated in the party. Even after dissent had been severely restricted, indeed virtually abolished, in March 1921, the party still continued to function as an institution, and some freedom of debate survived. Whatever the degree of his authority, Lenin never exacted the kind of adulation and submission which Stalin would exact, nor did he impede, let alone put an end to, the ordinary, constitutional functioning of the organs of the party.

The position became different after Stalin had inherited Lenin's power over the party. (Not his office—Lenin was never Secretary of the party. The elevation of the office of Secretary to the position of prime importance in the whole régime was Stalin's achievement, and the method by which he established his own power.) Stalin used the years between his first accession to power and the end of the purges (1938) to transform the party into something that was much more like a personal corps of adherents than a traditional party. He had faced and eliminated serious opposition in the party: his methods of doing so had been so drastic that virtually the entire party leadership was transformed. In the process of transforming the party well over a million members were executed or sent to labour camps, including the overwhelming majority of its top leaders. By 1939 the leading rôle in the party was being increasingly played by young men, recruited after 1929, who owed both their education and their advancement to the fact that they accepted Stalin's leadership without question, hesitation, or scruple. They were men for whom Lenin, the revolution and the Civil War were no more than legends. It would seem that until 1952 Stalin remained sufficiently confident of his control over the party not to repeat the operation of 1936–38: but the evidence suggests that just before he died he was contemplating a second, similar assault.

The characteristic feature of the party during Stalin's ascendancy was the fact that the institutional structure which had characterized it under Lenin declined. At the higher levels this was particularly evident in the atrophy of its normal organs: no party Congress met between 1939 and 1952, and the Central Committee was not summoned for years. In general, Stalin's style of rule was characterized by the way in which the rule through regular machinery (party, government apparatus) gave way increasingly to the rule of personal agents and agencies, each operating separately, and often in conflict, with Stalin in supreme overall control. The economic directors rose markedly in prestige: but Stalin was careful to ensure that their prestige at all times remained dependent on his own favour, and not on any institutional position which they enjoyed. The party Secretary remained the predominantly powerful man at the local level, at any rate up to 1938. But even here Stalin was careful to encourage what is the most distinctive feature of Soviet government—the local clique. This took (and takes) the form of an alliance at local levels of groups of leading officials in the party, the police, the administration, and so forth. This group, a local Mafia, enables power to be concentrated in a few hands, and others to be kept out: it cuts right across the established machinery. From the Leader's point of view it has the advantage that it prevents local machinery from growing too powerful. So far as the local Mafia is concerned he need have no fears, since he can at any time break it up by arrests and allow a new group to form. In this way it remained at all times evident that power derived not from the party or from any other institution, but from the favour of the Leader.

A somewhat comparable Mafia system prevailed at the top. Thus, neither at the local nor at the central level was the party, as an institution, allowed to maintain full control over the security organs. This control remained in Stalin's hands, and outside the machinery of the Central Secretariat, which is the general staff of the party. Within this Central Secretariat Stalin maintained a Personal Secretariat (probably identical with its 'Secret Department') which operated quite independently of the Central Secretariat. With the aid of the heads of this Personal Secretariat (which included Malenkov and the notorious Poskrebyshev as well as that of other personal agents, such as Vyshinsky), Stalin was able to keep control over this vital engine of terror without allowing it to acquire institutional power of its own.

These examples could be multiplied[14] but enough has been said to show that the party under Stalin, vital and important as it was as an instrument of rule and the repository of the traditional legitimacy (or what there was of it), was kept in a state of sufficient personal subjection to eliminate the danger of its becoming a rival in power to the Leader. This was no imaginary danger, so far as Stalin was concerned. During the period between 1934 and 1937 he faced a real danger from the party 'old guard' which, but for his drastic action, could well have achieved his own demotion from supreme power.[15]

Hitler's situation in this respect was different: his bloody, bold and resolute action against all potential opposition in June 1934 cowed his party, as well as the rest of the country, and seems to have assured him his ascendancy over the party until almost the very end. The party under Hitler acquired enormous power in different spheres of life: but, as in Stalin's case, the power remained that of individuals rather than that of an institution—and the individuals were plainly and manifestly dependent on the Leader's continuing favour. Hitler, says his biographer, 'hated the routine work of government, and, once he had stabilized his power' confined himself to general policy. 'In the Third Reich each of the party bosses, Göring, Goebbels, Himmler, and Ley, created a private empire for himself, while the Gauleiters on a lower level enjoyed the control of their own pashaliks. Hitler deliberately allowed this to happen; the rivalries which resulted only increased his power as supreme arbiter. Nobody ever had any doubt where the final authority lay—the examples of Roehm and Gregor Strasser were there, if anyone needed reminding. . . .'[16]

Examples of a similar kind could be drawn from Mussolini's relations with the Fascist Party. Mussolini's triumph after January 3, 1925 was as much a triumph over his opponents inside the party as over the remnants of parliamentary government. For the triumph was not that of Fascism, but that of Mussolini, and of Mussolini as Leader of state—not Mussolini as head of the party. Mussolini himself regarded the party as a kind of reserve of obedient and malleable robots. As the years went on, this optimism was scarcely justified, and conflicts with the party were a continual feature of Mussolini's chequered career as Leader. So far as the position on paper was concerned, the party was throughout intended to be clearly and unequivocally subordinated to the state, and to the Leader of the state, Mussolini, who was also president of the Grand Council of Fascism and, at any rate after the Party Statute of 1929, the official Commander of the Fascist Party, responsible for recommending to the king the appointment of the secretary of the party. But Mussolini never achieved supremacy of a kind comparable to that achieved by Hitler or Stalin and his weakness was reflected in his relations with the party as much as in his relations with the state, the Church and the courts.[17]

It is, perhaps, of interest that the tendency for one-party government to become leadership government was also illustrated in China under the Kuomintang: 'On examining and analysing the Kuomintang government, one gets the impression that it has been not so much a government by the Kuomintang, as a government by a group of men who have called themselves "Kuomintang" and who have all revolved around the Leader of the Kuomintang in the person of Chiang Kai-Shek.'[18]

Thus, the movement which, after capturing power, becomes the party is plainly a vital and important instrument of the Leader in the totalitarian régime. It is the repository of the ideology, and much of the legitimacy of the regime has to be built up by the ideologists in relation to the party's 'historic' or similarly mythological right to a position of pre-eminence and privilege. But it is evident that the successful Leader will not allow the party to become an institution which can rival his own supreme position: as far as possible he will try to ensure that the great authority of individual party members is clearly seen to derive from the Leader's support and favour, and not from the party as an institution. It is for this reason that descriptions of Germany under Hitler and of Russia under Stalin as 'one-party states' are completely misleading; while such descriptions as 'monopolistic' should be applied cautiously to the National Socialist or the Communist Party under Stalin, bearing in mind the qualification that the only real monopoly of power tolerated in the totalitarian polity is that of the Leader; and that the seeming 'monopoly' of the party's power is in fact nothing of the kind.

Church, state and society

There has already been occasion to mention the churches as a force for resistance within the totalitarian societies because they offer an alternative moral standard to the one offered by the Leader; and because thereby they can serve to bolster private morality against the onslaught of total rule. In one form or another, this question of the relation of church to secular power has dominated political thinking for centuries; but it has taken on a new significance since the emergence of totalitarian régimes. For it is evident that as controllers and manipulators of the ideology, the Leader and his ruling élite combine in the dominion of one man, or group of men, many of the powers of both church and state. As the historian of the 'Divine Right of Kings', Figgis, has so eloquently demonstrated, the rise of the claims of the secular ruler as against the claims of the church restored a balance between state and church, without which the liberty of the individual is gravely imperilled.

> The High Churchmanship of Bellarmin and Cartright led to the claim that only the adherence to the commands of the ecclesiastical authority could infuse that spirit of justice without which the Kingdoms of the world are but 'magna latrocinia'. . . . The opposite doctrine, that of the Divine Right of Kings . . . was historically the form in which the Civil State asserted its claim as a natural and necessary element in human life, and the independence of politics from merely ecclesiastical control. From both sides came elements of value to the modern world. . . . One view asserts the fundamental righteousness of the state apart from clerical interests, the other the necessity of recognizing other sides of life than the political, and of putting practical limits to the exercise of civil omnipotence. Where either aspect is neglected there is danger of tyranny—in the one case ecclesiastical, in the other secular.[19]

What happens in the 'totalitarian' system is that the boundaries between the two—the 'clerical interests' and the 'civil omnipotence'—are obliterated, and the two are fused. The 'clerical interests' of the ideology bolster the 'civil omnipotence' of the Leader and his system: the 'civil omnipotence' (always the primary consideration) is brought into play in order to further the 'clerical interests' of the ideology. It is small wonder that the totalitarian régime offered a pattern of tyranny of an extent and of a kind which the historian of Europe's sixteenth century could scarcely have imagined.

The analogy of church and state in the sixteenth century must not, however, be pushed too far. Whatever analogies may be drawn between the modern ideologies and religion (and they are often of doubtful validity) an ideology is not a church. A church, for one thing, is an institution with traditions, aims and an independence of its own: it is within the state, but it considers itself separate and apart from it, and only subject to it in a very strictly limited way. The ideology is an instrument of the Leader: it has no existence or force outside its function as a weapon in his hands. Indeed, the Leader, as propagator of the ideology, is, in a sense, himself 'the church' or a substitute for it; it is from this fact that his overwhelming power arises.

The church and state analogy is, however, false in another, and more important respect: if the Leader is a substitute for the church, but is not the church, it is even more the case that the Leader is a substitute for the state, but is not the state. The notion of the state conjures up in our minds first a pattern of system and regularity: it is the complex of powers and rights through which properly appointed and duly responsible officials exercise authority within spheres strictly delimited by law. Secondly, the state means, in common usage, a complex of offices, rather than of individuals: the right to exercise authority over others flows from the particular office, whoever the individual who fills it may happen to be: it is legal rather than personal authority. And thirdly, the notion of the state suggests regularity: the elements which make up the complex operate periodically, according to rules which are fixed and known, and which the holders of the various offices cannot transgress; or, if they do transgress them, can effectively be called to account.[19a]

Now, obviously not all states correspond to this pattern in every detail; nor would all theories of the state necessarily be in accord with what is implied in this description, that the notion of 'the state' is inseparable from the legal *authority* of the state, the legitimacy of the power of the state as well as its physical power to enforce its will. Kelsen, for example (as we saw), the extreme positivist theorist of law, rejected any notion of legitimacy as inherent in the notion of state: the authority of the state for him derives from the sole fact that it issues binding orders, and is obeyed. In this sense any system of rule, however arbitrary, however unpredictable, can be described as a state, and indeed such usage is not unknown. But it is the case that the more accepted usage, in the tradition of Western Europe at any rate, is to restrict the notion of 'state' to the condition described above, the coincidence of legal authority and of some regularity. It was in this sense that the classical theorists of politics, up till the nineteenth century, distinguished between a 'monarchy' and a 'tyranny': and the advocates of the most extreme and unlimited state power, such as Bodin and Hobbes, clearly distinguished between power which is naked power and nothing more, and authority, which is power clothed with the legitimate right of legal order. Hobbes, indeed, wrote his pamphlet *Behemoth* for the purpose of pointing the distinction, as the following extract from the dialogue (of which the pamphlet consists) shows:

> B. Now that there was no Parliament [i.e. after the dissolution of his last Parliament] who had the supreme power?
> A. If by Power you mean the right to govern, nobody had it: if you mean the supreme strength, it was clearly in Cromwell, who was obeyed as General of all the Forces in England, Scotland, and Ireland.

In what way was the position of Mussolini after January 1925, when he had finally routed the opposition in the Chamber; or of Hitler in 1933, after the proscription of the Communists and the Reichstag fire; or of Stalin, after the decimation of the party in 1938, different from Hobbes's estimate of Cromwell?

So far as Mussolini was concerned, he did not succeed in making very serious inroads into the state. This was probably in part due to the fact that it was through the state (in which the king remained nominal head) that Mussolini claimed, above all, to rule. No sooner had Mussolini fallen, than the kingdom (and the legal system), with little change, revived in the form in which it had managed to survive during the period when the Leader had tried to ride roughshod over it. It was indeed the case that Mussolini's 'totalitarian state', as he persisted in calling it, remained more 'state' than 'totalitarian'.

The position was very different under both Hitler and Stalin. Hitler's repeated conflicts with the law, and the dualism of arbitrariness and legality which resulted from them, have already been referred to. His conflicts with the state machinery which survived in large measure unimpaired even after his assumption of emergency powers (the Weimar Constitution remained technically in force throughout the National Socialist era) were even more bitter and prolonged. Hitler's views on the state are already quite evident in *Mein Kampf*. He scoffed at the 'really quite dog-like veneration' which Germans display for the state; and dismissed respect for the state authority for its own sake as 'madness and stupidity'.[20] His first action in the struggle with the state was to declare and enforce through the manipulative mechanism of the ideology the subordination of the state to the party. In this manner his own supremacy was best achieved, since inside the party he was successful in establishing his own supreme authority, and the dependence of the authority of every party member (which was considerable) on his own leave and license. The *Organization Handbook* of the NSDAP made the party-state relationship quite clear: 'It is the right and the task of the Party repeatedly to pump the vital spirit of the floods of its will into the state apparatus. The Party must . . . take care that it does not become too much interwoven with the State administrative machinery. Otherwise it runs the risk of being devoured by the bureaucracy of the State. . . .'[21] Actually, since the party was always in the position of acting with the Leader's authority, there was never much danger that it would not be able to enforce its will over the state in the last resort.

The way in which the arbitrary principle—exemplified by the Leader and the party—clashed with and successfully struggled against the state and to some extent also against the army, is amply illustrated in Dr Hans Buchheim's masterly study of the ss. The first stage in the struggle, the absorption by Himmler, as head of the ss, of actual authority over the regular police was a relatively simple matter. 'On 17 June 1936 by decree of the Führer and Chancellor, the Party post of Reichsführer ss [i.e. Himmler] was formally amalgamated with the newly created governmental office of Chief of the German Police. This was the all-important step in the transformation of the German Police into an instrument of the Führer's authority. . . .'[22]

But this was far from the end of the story: 'Time was required for the official character of the police and its internal and organizational regulations to be adapted to the very different forms and rules operative in the ss. Many aspects of police administration therefore remained unaffected, but they were allowed to continue only on a "subject to cancellation" basis. . . .'[23] The extension of the arbitrary, 'ideological' element in the whole police structure, until, in effect, it consumed what was left of the original legal, state structure, was the product of war and preparation for war: the methods justified by military necessity in occupied territories were extended to cover the whole of Germany. The incorporation of Austria and the Sudetenland in 1938 led to authorization to Himmler 'to take all necessary measures' for security 'even if these transgress the legal limits hitherto laid down for this purpose'.[24] The further expansion of Germany after 1939 led to an increasing area of arbitrary, uncontrolled, legally unlimited authority in the hands of Himmler and his subordinates, which cut right across civil and military administration, both within and outside Germany's pre-war boundaries.[25] The victory over the state was complete. In the end it was dictated by the very scale of National Socialist barbarity: the massacres of Jews, of Communists, of Poles and of Russians were by their nature so horrendous that even the orderly Germans could not be expected to carry them out within the make-believe of some legal framework. So the implementation of the Führer's policy became an act of ideological commitment rather than one of state routine. But though the scale may have been different after 1939, the principle of the 'ideological', as contrasted with the 'legal or bureaucratic', duty had obtained in Germany right from the moment when Hitler took power.

Enough has been said to show that to describe 'totalitarianism' in terms of the increasing encroachment by the state on society, or the like, as some authors have done, is completely to misunderstand what happened, at any rate in Germany and in Soviet Russia. It was not the state which increasingly absorbed society. It was the Leader and the apparatus of control which he created, or which operated under him, which progressively, like some evil cancer, ate their way into the fabric of *both* state *and* society. It was here that the real nature of the 'totalitarian' régime was revealed. The case of Germany is the most instructive in this respect, because in Germany one could observe two factors at their greatest strength: ideological deification of the Leader as distinct from the 'Party', or 'History', or some similar abstraction; and a tradition of law and of bureaucratic regularity of government which came into immediate conflict with the Leader who was above the law and above the state, both of which therefore had to be subjugated by him. One could not expect to find the same situation in Italy, where the power of the Leader never approximated to that of his German imitator; and where in any case his power ostensibly derived from the state. Even so, the much vaunted Corporative System, in so far as it was ever anything more than what Salvemini described as an elaborate piece of imposing humbug (and, one may add, corrupt humbug) was in essence an attempt to replace the machinery of parliament and state by a new form of extension of the Leader's control into the management of the national economy.[26]

The case of Stalin is again less instructive than that of Hitler, though for reasons which are quite different from those which make Mussolini's régime so much less illuminating on the nature of 'totalitarianism'. It has already been emphasized when discussing the nature of the Communist Party under Stalin, that his rule was above all personal, riding roughshod over or ignoring institutions of any kind. Obviously this included the machinery of the state—the Soviets, the courts, the trade unions, the government departments (People's Commissariats, later Ministries) the machinery of the Plan, and so forth. When necessary they could be, and were, used in order to put what was essentially the Leader's policy into operation. When necessary, as often happened, they could be side-tracked, and policy carried through by the party or by some other informally improvised group of Stalin's executants. But this was nothing new in Soviet experience: it had been going on, in one form or another, since 1917. The only real difference which Stalin had effected was so far as the party was concerned. If, under Lenin, the machinery of government was side-tracked and often treated as a façade, nevertheless the party, which was the real force behind the façade, remained an institution with a life and character of its own. Under Stalin even the party lost this institutional character, as Stalin increasingly asserted his personal domination over it. There was also a change of style. Lenin could still repeatedly and frankly stress the need for dictatorship—which he defined as naked force, unrestricted by any kind of law whatsoever. This, at all events, carried the implication of a temporary, emergency situation. Stalin, with more of an eye for the foreign observer perhaps, preferred to create in the constitution of 1936 which bears his name, an imposing façade of ostensibly permanent state machinery, with an ostensible legal framework. But state and the law were never any obstacle either to Lenin or to Stalin in the policies which they pursued: the opposition which each had to overcome was always mainly within the party.

Certain generalizations now appear to be justified. The 'totalitarian' régime is essentially a Leadership régime. Its ideology is in part a device to give the Leader the legitimacy which he lacks, and in part an instrument to be used in order to overcome the resistance which he would otherwise meet from both state and society. The Leader and his ruling apparatus thus find themselves in conflict with both the state and society. In this conflict the Leader is above all concerned to resist the natural tendency of the party or of the government machinery, or indeed of other institutions within society (the churches, for example), to preserve their institutional character, and hence their independence, since such independence would present a threat to the authority and ambitions of the Leader. The degree to which he is successful in his resistance to this tendency is the index of his prowess as 'totalitarian' Leader: both Hitler and Stalin, in this respect, were far more skilful than Mussolini. The essence of this conflict in which the Leader is engaged is that there arises a dualism of standards—the arbitrary and the legal, the prerogative and the routine, the ideological and the normal—or however it is thought best to describe it. The Leader must be victorious in this conflict in order to survive; and in the process of winning his victory the forms of rule which are associated with 'the state' and all that that entails, atrophy, or are left in abeyance, or are at all events overlaid by the Leader's apparatus of rule, which is quite distinct from the state. It follows that to speak of 'the totalitarian state' is to use a contradiction in terms; and it is for this reason that neutral terms, such as 'régime', have been used throughout this essay in preference to 'state', when referring to Fascist Italy, National Socialist Germany and Russia under Stalin.

4/How New Is Totalitarianism?

'Affinity' and 'Influence'

It was stressed at the outset that the emergence of a new political term does not of itself prove that the concept which it seeks to describe is also new. It is therefore necessary to explore the possibility that some kind of concept of a society corresponding to those whose 'contours' and 'pillars' have been described in the previous chapters already existed in the minds of men in the course of the long history of political thought.

This search for intellectual sources of political ideas raises an immediate problem: that of distinguishing what may be called intellectual 'affinity' from intellectual 'influence'. Direct 'affinity' may rightly be claimed where we can show that a genuine similarity in essential features exists between an earlier and a later thinker, justifying the conclusion that the two thinkers share in significant respects the same aim, the same outlook or the same values. It would, however, be wrong in such a case to assume that the later thinker was 'influenced' by the earlier, in the absence of outside evidence that this was indeed the case. All that can be established in such a case of 'affinity' is the existence in the history of thought of a recurrent tendency for the same problem to be resolved in similar fashion by men separated in time, but whose thought follows a similar pattern.

Conversely, where one can show that one man was directly influenced in his outlook by the writings of another, it by no means follows that a case of affinity has been established: the influence is often of a subjective kind in the sense that the man influenced has put his own interpretation on an idea torn out of context, or has consciously or unconsciously perverted the earlier thought.

The contrast can be clearly illustrated by two aspects of the development of Lenin's thought. There are a number of significant respects in which Lenin's thought can be shown to have been anti-cipated by the ideas of P. N. Tkachev, who died when Lenin was sixteen, in 1886. There is a close parallel in the two men's idea of the nature of a revolutionary élite and its organization, on the urgency of the need for revolutionary action before the autocracy could consolidate its hold by encouraging the development of a middle class, and on the need for the revolutionaries to preserve the machinery of the old state and to use it for their own purposes of reshaping society. Yet, the evidence that Lenin actually studied the writings of Tkachev is at best circumstantial.[1] This is a case of affinity. On the other hand, there is clear evidence that Lenin de-rived his key doctrine that revolutionary consciousness has to be injected into the proletariat from the outside by intellectuals from the writings of Karl Kautsky: yet this idea is only incidental to the thought of Kautsky, whose main ideas on revolution and socialism are in many respects opposed to and substantially different from those of Lenin.[2]

The importance of this distinction between affinity and influence will become evident below when the question of Rousseau, Hegel, and Marx as the originators of the 'totalitarian' idea is considered, in view of the fact that the affinity of these three has often been alleged by students of totalitarian society. Conversely, there are clear cases of influence, where it would be quite improper to deduce affinity from the known fact of direct influence alone—of Nietzsche on Mussolini and Hitler, for example, of Sorel and Pareto on Mussolini, or of Machiavelli on Mussolini and Stalin. Of course, there may well be cases where affinity and influence coincide, with-out the necessity of deducing the one from the other. Thus, we know that Mussolini was influenced at an important point of his career by Plato's *Republic*,[3] and it may well be contended that this is a case of both affinity and influence, in the sense that the relation of the individual to the hierarchy of rulers in Plato's vision has many similarities to that of the individual under the 'totalitarian' régime—as has been so forcibly argued by Sir Karl Popper in *The Open Society and its Enemies*.

In the following paragraphs some tentative guidelines are sug-gested along which a future study of the intellectual history of totalitarianism might be undertaken. But apart from tracing the history of the concept, it is also necessary to enquire to what extent the features which it has been suggested characterize the societies described as 'totalitarian' have been found in combination in the past. The remainder of the chapter will therefore be devoted to the outlines of such an enquiry.

The theorists of absolutism

Reasons were advanced in the last chapter for the view that it is erroneous to see the totalitarian régime as one in which the power of the state is advanced until it extends to the totality of all society and to the totality of each and every life. It was contended that, on the contrary, the state, with its rules and established order and institutions is as much the victim of the totalitarian all-pervasive cancer (which recognizes neither rules nor established order nor institutions), as are society and the individual. A state, in this sense, however powerful, may be oppressive in a high degree, but it cannot be 'totalitarian'. For whatever liberties are left to the individual outside of the extensive area over which the state asserts its powers can be enforced and defended as rights: in the totalitarian system, where law does not exist except in name, liberties, where they survive, or survive for some, are in the gift of the ruling *apparat*. If this contention is correct, it should follow that the great apologists of state power of the sixteenth and seventeenth centuries (when the notion of the secular state took root in men's minds) should not be regarded as in the line of intellectual affinity with the theorists and apologists of 'totalitarianism'. An examination of the view of three of the main advocates of the powerful state, Calvin, Bodin, and Hobbes, seems to bear out the view that they were all describing something quite different from the total power aimed at by Mussolini, and achieved by Stalin and Hitler.

Calvin is the least important of the three, so far as political thought is concerned. The section on political structure forms a very small part of his *Institutes*; his views are in general derivative, and consist of a familiar restatement of the duty to obey the secular authorities, and of the denial of any right to resist authority, supported by the customary scriptural texts. It is perhaps not too cynical to point out that since in Calvin's Geneva the church in fact dominated the state, and Calvin dominated the church, this was a doctrine which he could preach without in any way endangering his own or the church's authority. It was also the case (as will be noted below) that Geneva under Calvin's rule offers some parallels to the modern totalitarian prototypes. Nevertheless, even in Calvin's view there appears to be a clear distinction between the legal and the arbitrary—between the established, institutionalized authority of the state, however wide, and discretionary acts outside the law which must be inhibited if tyranny is to be avoided.

Thus, while the secular rulers, or magistrates, must be obeyed and may not be resisted, the happiest form of government is the one 'where liberty is framed with becoming moderation. . . .' Moreover, 'they do nothing at variance with their duty when they strenuously and constantly labour to preserve and maintain it'. Even the secular rulers, the magistrates, 'ought to do their utmost to prevent the liberty, of which they have been appointed guardians, from being impaired, far less violated. If in this they are sluggish, or little careful, they are perfidious traitors to their office and their country'. However, 'if from this you conclude that obedience is to be returned to none but just governors, you reason absurdly'. Their delinquencies are for divine, not secular retribution.[4] Nevertheless, in Calvin's day in Geneva 'divine retribution' (and fear of it) was no empty phrase. There is a world of difference between Calvin's magistrate and the totalitarian Leader.

But Calvin's influence was, perhaps, restricted in time and space. The fallacy of trying to search for intellectual affinity with totalitarianism among the advocates of strong government becomes more clearly apparent when we turn to the great, universal advocates of the absolute power of the state—Bodin and Hobbes.

Jean Bodin, in his *Six Livres de la Republique*, published in 1576, was primarily concerned to argue the case for strong, unchallengeable, secular, monarchical sovereignty. This sovereignty for him is indivisible: he who commands and has the power to issue laws is sovereign, and there the matter ends. But the contrast between Bodin's view of sovereignty and the kind of power claimed by the totalitarian Leader could hardly be more complete. In the first place, the absolutism advocated by Bodin is enlightened absolutism —he includes religious toleration, for example (Book IV, Chapter 7), and expresses doubts on the value of secular censorship (Book VI, Chapter 1). Moreover, the monarch, as distinct from the tyrant, rules in obedience to the law of God, and therefore respects the liberties of his subjects. Bodin is quite clear on what he means by a tyrant: 'A tyrannical monarchy is one in which the monarch tramples underfoot the laws of nature, in that he abuses the natural liberty of his subjects by making them his slaves, and invades the property of others by treating it as his own' (Book II, Chapter 4). Secondly, again in stark contrast to totalitarian rule, Bodin's monarchy, though legally absolute, is limited by tradition and by institutionalized and established interests which are respected and preserved. This is particularly evident in his attitude to estates and corporate associations. 'I hold that there is nothing that contributes more to the security of popular states and the ruin of tyrannies' than 'a moderate provision of estates, corporate associations and well-regulated communities. . . . To abolish all such societies is to embark on a barbarous tyranny, and so ruin the state. But it is also dangerous to permit all sorts of fraternities and assemblies whatsoever' (Book III, Chapter 7). [5] For the totalitarian Leader every independent institution within society is seen as a threat to his own dominant position.

It has already been pointed out that Thomas Hobbes distinguished clearly legitimate state power from naked force. It is the case that Hobbes's legitimate sovereign is endowed with greater powers than had probably ever been conceded to a sovereign in Western political thought. Nevertheless, there is a world of difference between Hobbes's sovereign and the 'totalitarian' Leader if only for one reason: the subject in Hobbes's polity retains his freedom in all cases where the law is silent, whereas the 'totalitarian' Leader recognizes no sphere whatever—be it legal, social, or moral—in which, by virtue of his rôle as Leader and by virtue of his pre-eminence as ideological guide, he cannot intervene. Under none of the three totalitarian régimes which have been considered could a subject ever enforce the proposition that what is not expressly forbidden is allowed. The legal principle *nulla poena, nullum crimen sine lege* was expressly repealed by Mussolini and by Hitler;[6] in the case of Stalin it had already been destroyed by Lenin.

The area of liberty envisaged by Hobbes is a good deal wider than might appear from the stern framework of the *Leviathan* (1651). In an early work *de Cive* (written in 1642) he concedes the right of disobedience where the sovereign commands acts of contumely against God, or prohibits worship of God, or decrees the worship of idols or the deification of men (xv, 18). The *Leviathan* is less explicit on matters of religon. But nonetheless the *Leviathan* permits civil disobedience in cases where the act enjoined by the sovereign 'frustrates the end for which the sovereignty was ordained', which is peace, protection, and order. It is not clear in all cases what commands Hobbes meant to include. But it is clear beyond doubt that the right of disobedience extended to a command to kill oneself, or not to resist those who assault one, or to incriminate oneself by confession (Part 2, Chapter 21). Besides, the area of silence of the law, within which liberty prevailed for Hobbes, was a wide one, and certainly of such an extent as to preclude any 'totality' of state power. 'The liberty of a subject, lieth therefore only in those things, which in regulating their actions, the sovereign hath praetermitted: such as is the liberty to buy, and sell, and otherwise contract with one another; to choose their own abode, their own diet, their own trade of life, and institute their children as they themselves think fit; and the like' (Ibid).

Nietzsche, Rousseau, Hegel, Marx

It is hoped that enough has been said to show that advocacy of strong, or absolute, state sovereignty is by no means identical with advocacy of the kind of totality of rule of which the three prototype régimes provided examples, and which their apologists such as Carl Schmitt and Gentile expounded. Nor is this surprising in the light of the evidence collected in the last chapter to show that Stalin and Hitler, at all events, were out to destroy the state rather than to bolster it, and to replace state rule by the rule of the Leader and his subordinate élite. It follows that to seek intellectual affinity with 'totalitarianism' in the thought of Bodin or Hobbes, or probably even of Calvin, is to misunderstand the nature both of the absolute state and of 'totalitarianism'. What is now proposed is to examine the thought of several men who can clearly be identified as having influenced one or more of the Leaders discussed in order to discover to what extent affinity coincides with influence. Let us first take the case of one where the affinity can be excluded, even though the influence on both Mussolini and Hitler is beyond dispute—that of Friedrich Wilhelm Nietzsche.

There is, of course, no doubt that the language and style of Nietzsche is in many respects that of Mussolini and Hitler: all three seem again and again to be extolling the same human types and virtues, and condemning what they see as the same human failings in the same voice of biting contempt. To list half a dozen of these similarities of thought and style is sufficient to prove this point. There is in the writings of Nietzsche contempt for Christianity and for the compassion which is part of it; and in general, dismissal of pity as 'the morality of the animal herd', and the 'morality of the slave revolt'. Again, 'the weak and the misbegotten must go to the wall. This is the first Commandment of our love for man.' Or again, the relegation of women to the sole function of breeding. One could also cite the denial by Nietzsche's Superman of any claim which the state may have to direct his way of life: the sole purpose of the state is to keep the mass in order, it is irrelevant for one who has the will to power. There is even reference in Nietzsche to the 'Lords of the Earth' as the future rulers of a Europe united under their sway.

One can see that statements of this kind were heady stuff for the would-be Nordic Lords of the Earth under the spell of Goebbels and Himmler, or to the Neapolitan mountebanks masquerading as patricians of ancient Rome. But for all that, to identify the thought of Nietzsche with Fascism and National Socialism is to do violence to intellectual history. For Nietzsche is above all an individualist, who would have completely rejected the totalitarian view of the individual's place in the community. Again, Fascism is nothing if not a mass movement. Mussolini and Hitler may have despised the masses whom they could manipulate. But it was an essential part of their doctrine that their rule was for the benefit of the masses, and was based on the support and love of the masses. This is not remotely related to anything that Nietzsche (who incidentally was also scathingly critical of German anti-Semitism and German nationalism) was concerned with. There was, in truth, little in common between the mad philosopher and the mad demagogue except violence of language.

Let us now turn to three cases where the influence is also beyond doubt, but where the affinity is more debatable: Rousseau, Hegel, and Marx, each of whom has frequently been held up as the father of modern totalitarianism. It is strange that Rousseau, a passionate defender of liberty and the symbol of liberty in much of French thought today, should be of this company. What theorist of totalitarianism could ever have written such lines as these: 'Liberty consists less in doing one's own will, than in not being subject to the will of another. . . . There can therefore be no liberty without laws, nor in any case where any one man is above the law. . . . A people is free, whatever the form of its government, when it sees its rulers not as men but as agents of the law.'[7]

When, however, he came to write the *Social Contract*, published in 1762, he became, as it were, hypnotized by the solution which he had devised in order to ensure man's freedom. This solution was that man should govern himself: his freedom would then be assured, since no man is likely to try to enslave himself. But since for Rousseau, the citizen of a city state, nothing but direct self-government would do; and since in a large community direct self-government is impossible, Rousseau became enmeshed in an abstraction, the 'general will' and failed to discern that the Utopia which he proposed, and in which he provided no safeguards for the individual against the state (why should a man need safeguards against himself?) could lead to the most complete tyranny. Thus, 'sectional associations' must be prohibited in order not to impede the clear expression of the general will (Book II, Chapter 3); representative government must be discarded as an impossibility (Book III, Chapter 15); and a civil religion, displacing Christianity, must be imposed by force (Book IV, Chapter 8).

These, and more, can well be described as essential aspects of totalitarian thought and practice.[8] It is probably true that nowhere so much as in the *Social Contract* is the danger so clearly apparent of what happens when a man is carried away with enthusiasm for some overall blue-print which is to solve all the problems of mankind at one stroke; or perhaps one should say of what can happen when those who fall under the influence of the writer concerned endeavour to put his ideas into practice. The fact remains that there is little doubt that Rousseau would have been horrified at the sight of his prescriptions in the *Social Contract* being ostensibly carried out by the Committee of Public Safety. Perhaps the most generous verdict on Rousseau remains that of Benjamin Constant, who was certainly no admirer of the Jacobin dictatorship:

> I am far from joining Rousseau's detractors: they are pretty numerous at this moment. . . . He was the first to popularize the feeling for one's rights; it was to the sound of his voice that the most generous hearts and the most independent spirits were awakened. But he did not know how to define with precision those things which he so powerfully felt.[9]

Hegel is another philosopher whose direct influence on the apologists and ideologists of totalitarianism can hardly be doubted. For the purpose of this essay our enquiry must be limited to the influence of Hegel's theory of the state: it is not possible here to pursue the broader question of the influence of Hegel's general philosophy of history on the philosophy of totalitarianism. Indeed the influence of Hegel has been so widespread and so significant that merely to discuss it is to study the whole intellectual history of Europe.[10] But the charge against Hegel as the spiritual father of totalitarianism is often based on his view of the state, and of the individual's relation to it—a view which was certainly at the basis of Gentile's philosophy of Fascism.

Now there is no doubt that in Hegel's *Philosophy of Right* the state is given a position of ethical primacy. It is 'mind on earth, consciously realizing itself there'. It is 'the march of God in the world . . .' and its basis is 'the power of reason, actualizing itself as will' (p. 279). Hegel is careful to emphasize throughout that he is dealing with the 'Idea' of the state rather than with any particular state. It was within this state, and only within this state, that Hegel saw it as possible for the individual to fulfil himself. 'In the course of the actual attainment of selfish ends . . . there is formed a system of complete interdependence, wherein the livelihood, happiness, and legal status of one man is interwoven with the livelihood, happiness, and rights of all. On this system, individual happiness etc. depend, and only in this connected system are they actualized and secured. This system may be *prima facie* regarded as the external state . . .' (p. 123). Moreover, it is only in the state that the individual can achieve freedom at all: 'The state is absolutely rational inasmuch as it is the actuality of the substantial will which it possesses in the particular self-consciousness once that consciousness has been raised to consciousness of its universality. This substantial unity is an absolute, unmoved and in itself, in which freedom comes into its supreme right. . . . Since the state is mind objectified it is only as one of its members that the individual himself has objectivity, genuine individuality, and an ethical life' (pp. 155–6).

Since the Prussian state, and for that matter the state apparently envisaged by Hegel, was quite undemocratic and certainly very extensive in its powers, a parallel has been drawn by some critics between Hegel's doctrine and that of the totalitarian apologists. This seems erroneous. However extensive the powers of Hegel's state may be, it remains poles apart from the *apparat* which exercises rule in the totalitarian régime in at least three respects. It is based on law, not on arbitrary force; its powers, however extensive, are definite and circumscribed; and it allows both tolerance and the separation of church and state (pp. 165–74). Indeed, Hegel, in a passage devoted to the superseded 'world-historical realm' of the oriental despotism, specifically condemns a form of government based on personal power and tradition rather than law, which in the form in which he describes it is very close to the modern totalitarian system—if 'ideology' is substituted for 'religion' in the following quotation. It is 'theocratic', the ruler is 'also a high priest or God himself; constitution and legislation are at the same time religion, while religious and moral commands, or usages rather, are at the same time natural and positive law'. In default of laws, government consists of 'unwieldy, diffuse, and superstitious ceremonies, the accidents of personal power and arbitrary rule. . . . Hence in the Oriental state nothing is fixed, and what is stable is fossilized . . .' (p. 220).[11]

While Hegel can therefore be excluded from affinity with the totalitarian concept because of his championship of the state based on law, the same reasoning can clearly not be applied to Marx, since for Marx both the state and law are no more than the phenomena of the class society, destined to disappear in the future classless society. The case for including the doctrine of Marx in the intellectual genealogy of totalitarian theories can be put in two ways.

In the first place it can be argued that the classless society envisaged by Marx, where government will be replaced by self-administration, in which neither force nor law will play any part, is a chimaera; and that if it were ever realized, or the attempt were made to realize it, the result in practice could only be oppressive and arbitrary rule in which the individual would have neither the state, with clearly defined limits of power, to protect him, nor the law to stand between him and the state. In this sense it can be said that Marx erred in a way very similar to that of Rousseau—Rousseau in failing to see that the individual will always need protection against the state, even where the state is ostensibly his 'own' state; and Marx in failing to foresee that the individual would require protection against something called 'administration' even more than he requires it against the 'state'. The second reason for seeing in Marx one of the fathers of totalitarianism is based on what happened in practice in Russia in 1917 and after. However much Lenin's views may have owed to an indigenous Russian revolutionary tradition, they were certainly to a large extent derived from Marx. Yet, the attempt by Lenin to put his doctrines into practice certainly laid the foundations for the totalitarian régime in Russia created by Stalin, even if it is true that Russia under Lenin should not itself be described as totalitarian.

Both these arguments seem to me to be equally fallacious, and for the same reason. Marx, unlike Lenin, did not conceive of the classless society of the future as something that would have to be created, but as a stage in the dialectical movement of history. When that stage was reached, as he believed it would ineluctably be reached in the process of the development of capitalist society, the very basis of the existence of law, government, and the state—exploitation, class conflict, and man's alienation from his work—would have disappeared. This higher phase of society could never be achieved by conscious acts. If, in the course of the working out of the dialectical law, the proper stage had been reached, some force might be needed (though not always necessarily) during a short transitional period—the period of the 'dictatorship of the proletariat' to which Marx on a few occasions referred. If it had not been reached, no amount of force could bring it about. It was for this reason that Marx was scathing in his criticism of the Jacobin dictatorship. It was also for this reason that Marx never used the term 'wither away' with reference to the state—the term was popularized by the much less subtle Engels. For 'withering away' suggests a gradual process, beginning with a revolution—as is evident in the interpretation put on these words by Lenin in his *State and Revolution*. The term used by Marx is 'transcended' (*aufgehoben*), which is more consistent with his philosophical and dialectical interpretation of the course of human society.[12]

What Lenin did was precisely to try to bring about by conscious action the classless society, at a time when Russian society was very far from ripe for it—as indeed Lenin admitted in a number of his writings in the last months of his active life.[13] Countless Marxist critics of Lenin before the revolution had foretold that the result of such an attempt could only result in a dictatorship by the revolutionary élite. What is quite certain is that the result would not have caused Marx any surprise. Marx's views of the dialectics of history may be right or wrong—the question is in this context immaterial. It is, no doubt, the case that the misuse of his doctrine by impatient revolutionaries who failed to understand them, or deliberately misunderstood them, led straight on to the totalitarian form of Communist rule as we know it in this century. But to trace the origins of totalitarian doctrine to Marx is once again to do violence to intellectual history.

'Left' and 'Right'

It seems desirable at this point to add a short excursus on the distinction which is sometimes made between 'left' and 'right' totalitarianism—with the Communist variety placed on the 'left', and the Fascist on the 'right'. There are probably no two terms in the language of politics which are more imprecise and subjective in the meanings which are attached to them than 'left' and 'right', and which are more misleading in their common usage. Now, if one derives the variety which calls itself 'Communist' from Rousseau and Marx, and the 'Fascist' kind from Hegel and Nietzsche as well as the purveyors of racialist and anti-Semitic claptrap whose writings went to form Hitler's outlook,[14] then it can be argued that the one is revolutionary, and therefore 'left', and the other conservative, or reactionary, and therefore 'right'. Reasons have already been advanced for the view that these derivations are of doubtful validity; and it has been contended that influences must not be confused with affinity.

Nor does it seem sound to base the distinction on a difference of tradition. Totalitarianism of the 'left', it has been argued, takes man as its central point: on the 'right' the collective entity—the race, or the state—is the dominant theme. It is for this reason that the one is universal in its aims, while the other is restricted in its ultimate aim. Moreover, it is said, the 'left' starts from the assumption that man is essentially good and perfectible: the 'right' believes man to be weak and corrupt.[15]

This argument breaks down the moment the distinction is drawn between affinity and influences, and the consequent confusion avoided. In what sense can man be said to be the central point in Stalin's, or even Lenin's Russia, with its overwhelming emphasis on class, on party and on the community, and its total disregard of the individual in the process? Nor is the distinction true in terms of universality. Hitler's version of the future, with the 'Ayrans' led by the Germans dominating the inferior races was nothing if not universal. It can certainly be argued that Lenin believed in the essential goodness and perfectibility of man. But Stalin? To pose the question is to answer it. In short, there is every reason to study both the similarities and the differences between the various totalitarian societies which exist or have existed, since each is, or has been, distinct and peculiar. But there is no illumination to be derived from the misleading 'Left–Right' classification.

The Utopians

Assuming, then, that it is correct to argue that there is no direct line of affinity between either the theorists of absolutism or Rousseau, Hegel and Marx on the one hand, and the theorists or apologists of totalitarianism on the other, where then is the affinity to be sought? It seems that there has been evident for many centuries in Europe a line of thought on the organization of human society which has many points of resemblance to 'totalitarianism'. This is the type of theorizing about politics usually called Utopianism. What all thinkers of this temperament share is some vision of a polity designed according to a plan, or blueprint, which pays no regard to society as it is, to its historical origins and the practical limits of possible evolution. Such thinkers propound the virtues of a society in every way different from any known or actual one, indeed often propound their ideal society with the specific object of exposing by way of stark contrast the vices which they see in their own or in other contemporary societies. Another feature which Utopian thinkers share is a belief in the need for a complete transformation of human nature, whether this need is expressly argued, or is left to be implied from the kind of ideal society which they describe, in which human failings and weaknesses which have been evident throughout the ages have no place, or have somehow ceased to exist.

But these common features apart, there is much variety in Utopian thinking. In particular, there is the broad division between those writers who dwell in detail on the exact way in which the ideal society is to be governed, and prescribe the means, educational or penal, by which human nature is to be transformed; and those who either pass this question over in silence, or dismiss it lightly on the basis of some assumption which is treated as axiomatic.

As an example of the first category one may cite Plato's *Republic*. Although it is true that the *Republic* must be read within the corpus of Plato's philosophy as belonging to the realm of the ideal rather than the actual, it is none the less true that the *Republic* presents a picture of total and drastic regimentation, in which the liberty of the individual plays no part: education, hierarchical rule by an élite, control over occupation and thought are all provided for in detail, which must strike chords of apprehension in the hearts of those who have seen much of this kind of prescription put into practice in the twentieth century with the ostensible aim of building an ideal society and a new man to inhabit it.

Among those who pass the question of means over lightly may be cited William Morris in *News from Nowhere*. The delightful society there depicted was intended by the author as a popular exposition of Marxism as he saw it, and he was little concerned with the means by which it would be attained. No doubt he took it for granted (as Marx took it for granted) that the advent of the classless society and the end of private property would of themselves bring about the transformation of human nature and human relations which *News from Nowhere* depicts. Another such example is the 'withering away' of government and its replacement by 'administration' depicted by Lenin in *State and Revolution*. No doubt Lenin had persuaded himself in September 1917 that the imminent seizure of power by the Bolsheviks would inaugurate the start of a new era. Within months of the October *coup d'état* Lenin was talking in very different terms about the supposed imminent 'withering away' of the state;[16] and by the end of his active life he recognized that the Bolshevik revolution bore little relationship to the kind of socialist revolution that Marx had envisaged.

Two moments in modern Utopian thought in Europe seem to be particularly relevant to the study of affinity in intellectual history with modern totalitarian doctrines: eighteenth-century French rationalist thought; and the doctrines of Saint-Simon. A whole library could, no doubt, be filled with the works of writers in eighteenth-century France who set down, often in semi-fictional form, their dream of an ideal society, implicit in which was criticism of their own society.[17] But one of the most representative and most influential, Morelly's *Code de la Nature*, published in 1755, is of especial interest for two reasons. First, because Morelly, like Marx, saw the source of all evil in private property. Unlike Marx, however, he did not see the solution of the problem as a dialectical one in which *both* private property *and* the social and political organization based upon it would be 'transcended', and thus cease to be relevant. For Morelly the liberation of man is to be achieved in the Jacobin way, which Marx so strongly deplores—the deliberate acts of men in authority over others. Small wonder, therefore, that Morelly's *Code* propounds, with the most noble intentions, what de Tocqueville summarized a hundred years after its publication as 'Common ownership of property, the right to work, absolute equality, uniformity in all things, mechanical regularity in all human actions, tyrannous regimentation and the complete absorption of the personality of the citizen in the social body.' The second reason for selecting Morelly as an example is the influence which he may be supposed to have exercised in the Soviet Union. Three editions of the *Code* in translation appeared in the course of twenty-five years.[18]

Whether or not Morelly should properly be described as Utopian, since his most influential work (as distinct from his earlier *Basiliade*) is not cast in the conventional semi-fictional style, there is no doubt of the great debt which he owed to Sir Thomas More's *Utopia*. But he is also believed to have been influenced by a work on the civilization of the Incas (which, as suggested below, displays many totalitarian features) by Garcilaso de la Vega, published in Madrid in 1608, and in French translation in 1633.[19] The burden of the *Code*, of which only the fourth, and smallest, section is devoted to the laws which are to govern Morelly's ideal society, is that man is by nature good, but corrupted by greed, which in turn derives from private ownership of property which is contrary to the laws of nature. Natural life is based not on property, but on mutual interdependence. The object of legislation should be to restore this state of affairs in human society. Private property is therefore to be abolished: each citizen will live at public expense, and will in turn contribute according to his ability to the public weal.

This is the first, short section of the code of legislation. The remaining eleven sections deal with every aspect of life, regulating it at every stage and aspect, ordering everything, forcing everything into a symmetrical pattern: the cities are uniform, married life is strictly controlled, education is minutely prescribed. Philosophy is confined within rigid limits, the fine arts somewhat less so. (It may be observed that Morelly showed a good deal more sense than

Stalin in providing for unlimited freedom in research in the applied sciences.) This planned paradise is enforced by drastic penal laws. Machinery of government is paternalistic and pyramidal. It is based on division into families, tribes, cities, and provinces, and, in the case of the different crafts and professions, on units of ten. To each unit of work is assigned its 'master', who is also the police informer to the next tier of professional organization. Each pater-familias over fifty is a senator, each family in turn provides a tribal chief, each town in turn a city chief. Subordinate senates of cities are controlled by the Supreme Senate. At the head of the state is the General. It would seem that the pyramid of senates was intended to be both legislature and judicature. At all events, there is no mention in the *Code* of judges, or of any means available to the citizen to protect himself against those set over him. For Morelly believed that with private property once abolished, the human failings which lead to tyranny and abuse of power would likewise disappear.

Saint-Simon, like Morelly, is the supreme planner and organizer of men, but, unlike Morelly, does not see the need for any compulsion in the process. On the contrary, such is the power of man's rational judgement that if once he is shown the supremely rational order which Saint-Simon was proposing for him, his reason would of its own accord lead him to accept it. Because of this it is perhaps wrong to classify Saint-Simon as an Utopian, in the sense that Morelly, who did not really believe that his ideal society was possible of achievement,[20] was an Utopian. Indeed, Saint-Simon vigorously denied that he was an Utopian, and there is no evidence that he ever read Plato's *Republic*, or Sir Thomas More's *Utopia*.[21] Again, unlike Morelly, who was indifferent to individual liberty, Saint-Simon was so far convinced of the rational and benevolent nature of the society which he envisaged as desirable, that he believed that it was only in such a society that each individual could really attain the fullest development suitable to his talents and inclinations.

If Morelly was a High Priest, Saint-Simon was above all a Manager, an apostle of efficiency. He regarded poverty as the main enemy to be overcome: and in his view the greatest evil which can

befall a society is disorder. Order, welfare, efficiency, prosperity—
these are his keynotes. The industrial class, headed by its élite of
managers and supported by the workers, was to achieve the kind of
'industrial régime' which he saw as desirable: the sole criterion for
all laws and acts of administration would be—Are they useful or
harmful to industry?[22] He regarded religion as a particularly useful
'human invention', since it was the only 'political institution' which
has as its aim 'the general organization of humanity'[23]—in proper
hands, no doubt. He despised parliamentary democracy and had
little use for freedom of speech or thought, largely because they
were frivolous and irrelevant to the main issue of industrial pro-
gress and efficiency. He saw as his main mission in life the persuading of the leaders of industry, the enterpreneurs, to assume the rôle
in society for which they were, as he believed, destined. He was less
explicit on the precise way in which the administration of the
future would be carried out, though he did on at least one occasion
lay down the outlines of a three-chamber administration. In this
scheme the artists and engineers would make the plans and explain
them, the scientists would examine the plans and control education
but the final chamber alone, consisting of the leaders of industry,
would approve plans and put them into execution.[24] Saint-Simon
is even more cavalier than Rousseau on the question of protecting
the individual against the government. The fear, he says, of a despotism emerging where government is in the hands of men of
science and industry is 'a chimaera as ridiculous as it is absurd'.[25]

It is no part of the argument of this essay that Plato, Morelly or
Saint-Simon was a forerunner of the totalitarian doctrines of the
twentieth century. All that is contended is that their preoccupation
with ends and indifference to means, or indifference to the effect of
the means proposed by them on the liberty of the individual; the
totality with which they view man and his place in society; the firm
and dogmatic assumptions on which they based their political prescriptions; their preoccupation with management and direction,
and their ignoring of the variety of human character and experience;
and the confidence with which they wished to see their blueprints
put into practice—all bring their views closer than any others
which have been considered hitherto to the totalitarian theories

which were built up around Mussolini, Hitler, or Stalin. These Utopians are 'dirigistes'—which Marx was not; and, in contrast to both Hobbes and Hegel, they have no time in their search for total management for the diversification, limitation, and circumscription of law, institutions, and the state.

Yet in one respect these Utopians part company with totalitarianism: their theories are not in any sense clothed in the trappings of democracy, the legitimacy of their élites is based on moral pre-eminence, reason, or utility to industry. In no conceivable sense do they pretend, as all totalitarian leaders have pretended, that legitimacy of rule should be derived from the investiture of mass approbation and adulation; and totalitarian doctrines are nothing if not democratic in their pretensions. If, therefore, totalitarianism of the twentieth century is to that extent a new concept, one would expect to find that in practice the three societies with which we are concerned are without their exact counterparts in history. To this question it is now necessary to turn.

A search for historical parallels

Tyrannous and oppressive government is as old as mankind. In the Fifth Book of the *Politics*[26] Aristotle describes in detail the methods which tyrants should adopt if they wish to be successful and the description could hardly be improved on by Hitler or Stalin. He sums up the main aims of a tyrant as '(1) to breed mutual distrust among their subjects, (2) to make them incapable of action, and (3) to break their spirit'. Equally useful hints could be, and probably in some cases were, gleaned by modern tyrants from Thucydides, Tacitus, Suetonius, Machiavelli, Bodin, and a score of other writers. But the tyrants with which these writers were concerned were primarily anxious to preserve themselves in power, and to advance their personal interest: their tyranny did not as a rule extend to the mass of the population beyond ensuring that they would have little chance of revolting.

The prototype Leaders were quite different in this respect: they were determined to mobilize the population, for war or for some other end. They aimed at transforming the men and women over whom they ruled into something new, and to this end pressed

something which they called 'ideology' into service, and sought
with its help to invade every corner of human life and activity.
Lastly, they claimed the right to do all this on the basis of a legitimacy which at any rate as one of its elements included mass approbation, and used their 'ideology' as an instrument for winning and
holding this mass approbation. If therefore parallels are to be
sought in past societies to the three prototype societies of the present century, something more than tyrannous government must be
looked for which must at least include the three further elements
listed above. It would seem that in the vast literature which exists
on the subject of totalitarianism no completely parallel instances
which exhibit all these three characteristic features have hitherto
been discovered. A few examples only can be examined here.

To a superficial observer ancient Sparta may seem to offer some
parallel with the modern totalitarian régimes. The similarity is
suggested by the militarism of Sparta and by the severity of train-
ing and conditioning which the state exacted from the young of
both sexes, reminiscent of National Socialist Germany. On examination, however, the superficial parallel proves to be completely
false. The Greeks of the classical period were fully aware of the
difference between the tyranny and the constitutional state: for
them, and rightly, Sparta belonged to the latter category. Sparta
was not, like Athens, a democracy (a 'polity', in Aristotle's classification) but an oligarchy, governed on a strictly legal pattern,
normal for Greece, and sharply distinguished by the Greeks from
tyranny, which was regarded as an exceptional, arbitrary, highly
undesirable and pathological political condition.[27] Sparta indeed
attracted admiration for the stability of her constitution which
enabled her (except for a short period) to avoid the scourge of
tyranny. The main elements of the Spartan constitutions—the two
kings, the Council of Elders, the popular assembly and the executive consistory of five ephors functioned regularly and performed
their discrete and separate functions under the rule of law.[28] However severe the laws may have been, there can therefore be no possible parallel to the rule of the totalitarian Leader and his minions
which deliberately undermines and subverts the law, the constitution and the regular institutions of government.

In this respect, the parallel of the tyrant in the classical world is, of course, much closer. For the tyrant subverts the constitution to the end of his personal aggrandizement and, when once in power, rides roughshod over both the law and the populace who have in their unwisdom, helped him to achieve power. In classical times the term 'tyrant' was in fact a pejorative word for a ruler who usurped power and destroyed the constitution; and 'tyranny' was regarded as the greatest evil which could befall a polity. But again the parallel cannot be pushed too far, since the classical tyranny lacks many features characteristic of the totalitarian régime, such as an ideology, a party or movement, or mobilization of the population towards some Utopian end.[29]

The empire of the Incas (which, it will be recalled, may have influenced Morelly when writing his *Code de la Nature*) is the first important example of an ancient pre-industrial society which exhibits many features of totalitarianism. In the first place it was completely theocratic, in the sense that the ruler was divine, and controlled both secular affairs and the priesthood.[30] Moreover, the state religion was used as an 'ideology', at any rate for the purpose of persuading the population that what was really a policy of taxing the poor in order to reward the influential men who could bolster the ruler, was a policy of social welfare. There was total mobilization of national effort for state works and for military purposes. On the other hand, those who were engaged on the state *corvée* were housed and fed by the state, and they were the great majority. There was also a system of community-supported labour at lower levels than the state level.[31] Moreover, 'despite a not inconsiderable technical development, Inca society developed no conspicuous, independent private-property-based classes. The sinecure lands, which the Incas assigned to certain members of the ruling group, created no full-fledged ownership; and professional private enterprises were virtually absent in the sphere of transport and trade, which in other civilizations favoured the rise of independent rich merchants.'[32] Here then we find the fusion of church and state, ideological control, even if rudimentary, total mobilization of labour and the absence of independent private property to act as a bulwark against state power. It is probably one of the closest parallels from the past, but it lacks one essential element: there is little if any mobilization of mass support and enthusiasm; and there is no question whatever of the ruler's divine legitimacy seeking validity in the approbation of the masses. The empire of the Incas was a managerial autocracy: it was therefore different from the totalitarian mass societies of the twentieth century.

Theocracy, or fusion of church and state in one ruler or ruling élite, is, of course, a salient feature of the totalitarian régime. There were many examples of this type of rule in the ancient world. But two examples from more modern times of so-called theocracies are instructive in order to point the distinction from the totalitarian systems: Byzantium, and Geneva during the period of Calvin's ascendency (1555–64). The enormous and, in theory, unlimited powers of the Byzantine emperor and the 'Caesaro-papism' under which the emperor headed a church which was essentially a state institution might at first sight tempt one to draw some kind of parallel with the totalitarian régimes. But the parallel is completely erroneous. Whatever else it may have been, the Byzantine empire was founded on an elaborate legal system. The church, though theoretically subordinate to the emperor, could and did impose its will on the emperor in matters of faith and morals—to the extent even of excommunicating an emperor on two occasions. The emperor's liberty of action was in many ways bound both by tradition and by the law; nor was he able easily to override his own bureaucracy in cases of conflict. A powerful commercial and land-owning class was able to retain a degree of independence.[33]

Calvin's Geneva is a similarly false parallel—quite apart from its very small scale and its short duration. For some ten years Calvin exercised enormous powers over the life of Geneva through the Consistory, formed of the Company of Pastors and the Elders of the Church, with ill-defined but very widespread powers. The activity of the Consistory extended to the control of private morality and to the preservation of religious beliefs. It acted with the aid of a network of informers. It effectively dominated the civil power, at any rate after 1560, by a form of electoral manipulation based on prohibition of discussion of political matters except in the presence of the Council, which was effectively 'packed'. Against these and other seemingly totalitarian features must be set the fact that all this took place within a small community dominated by religious fanaticism, which called for nothing comparable to the 'ideological' manipulation which was required in the modern totalitarian prototypes. More important, Calvin's régime left virtually untouched the important areas of banking and commerce—a fact which earned Calvin a severe reproof from Mably. One should add to this list of differences that there was no real attempt at mobilization of the population in Geneva and the fact that the basis of legitimacy was aristocratic rather than democratic.[34]

It is easy to find elements of totalitarianism in many of the polities of the past four centuries in Europe—in Tudor England for example, with its travesty of legal procedure, or its rigged political trials; or in Muscovite Russia with its virtual lack of a legal order and its extensive system of police terror. But these parallels are emotional and superficial: to apply the term 'totalitarian' to every form of morally reprehensible government is to render the term useless. These and other instances of past tyrannies lack both mobilization and mass legitimacy. Moreover, their influence did not normally extend beyond a narrow circle. The bulk of the population was left alone in its poverty so long as it made no attempt to rebel.

The most important and comprehensive study of historical parallels with the modern totalitarian régimes is that undertaken by Karl A. Wittfogel, whose work on *Oriental Despotism* has already been referred to. Wittfogel analysed the way in which the rule which was exercised in the 'hydraulic' societies for the purpose of mobilizing large masses of the population for public works of irrigation, or the like, becomes political leadership: those who control the network necessary for the management of public works 'are uniquely prepared to wield supreme political power'.[35] This leads to infinitely greater control by the ruler over agriculture and construction than was known either in the Greek city states or in medieval Europe. The reason for this is that the managerial apparatus which is required for mammoth hydraulic and similar constructions prevents the non-governmental forces in society from crystallizing into independent forces strong enough to counterbalance the political machine.[36] Private property is thus restricted through fiscal and political measures, and 'nowhere in hydraulic society did the dominant religion place itself outside the authority of the state as a nationally (or internationally) integrated autonomous church'.[37]

These are important and illuminating parallels. But there are also important contrasts. There is, of course, no question of mass legitimacy: the rulers wield traditional authority, their title is divine or hereditary. Nor do they seek to mobilize mass support or enthusiasm. Their aim is managerial, not Utopian. They show no desire to transform human nature and to create a 'new man', or the like. So long as they can keep themselves supplied with the labour which they need for their plans, they are content to let the mass of the population alone in what Wittfogel calls its 'Beggar Democracies'. One could add that they lack the technical means of communications and weapons which play so significant a rôle in the assertion by the totalitarian Leaders of their power.[38]

It would be presumptuous to base a conclusion on so cursory an exposition of the evidence were it not for the fact that it is warranted by the work of scholars who have devoted themselves to the question. The conclusion is that nowhere in the records of the history of mankind can we find a society which exhibits all the characteristic features which were observable in the prototype totalitarian societies. More particularly, in the totalitarian societies, and nowhere else in the past, we are dealing with what is essentially an aspect of mass democracy, in turn a phenomenon of the twentieth century. The authority of the Leader is always pseudo-democratic in form—the plebiscite, the fake election, the adulation, the mass meeting, the endless reiteration of slogans, the ceaseless bombardment of the population in the press and by radio, the indoctrination. There is no parallel to all this in the experience of the past because it was something which could only be produced in a period when man was persuaded that the old order and the old hierarchies had broken down, that the needs and wishes of the mass of the population were paramount; and that the sole legitimacy of a ruler could be his acceptance as ruler by the mass of the population. That the mass of the population of Italy, Germany and

Russia was repeatedly hoodwinked, exploited and deceived by its Leaders in the name of mass democracy is quite irrelevant to the issue. But, it should also not be forgotten that along with the sufferings and deprivations went a certain amount of *panis et circenses*, and that both under Mussolini and Hitler, and under Stalin, there were always some formerly deprived sections of the population who could believe with some justification that their interests had at long last been served.

Thus, it would seem to be justifiable to conclude that both as a concept and as a way of life totalitarianism is something new in the history of mankind, new precisely because it has grown up in 'the age of the democratic revolution'—to use Palmer's masterly phrase. It is for this reason that one seeks in vain in the past records of political thought for true affinity with totalitarian theory. There were, however, some who had the prescience to realize that there was inherent in the democratic society of the future a danger to which they gave no name, but which can be discerned as a foreboding of totalitarianism. Dostoevsky's *Legend of the Grand Inquisitor* expresses just such a foreboding—that the mass of men will in the end accept despotism in return for security and in order to gain release from the burden of responsibility which freedom imposes on man.

The man whose foreboding came very close to what in fact was to come about was Alexis de Tocqueville. Writing in 1839 or 1840, under the impact of his study of democracy as it was developing in America, he says:

> I think therefore that the forms of oppression which threaten democratic peoples will in no way resemble the forms of oppression which have hitherto been known. . . . Try as I will, I cannot find a phrase which will render with precision the conception which I have formed of this oppression . . . the old words 'despotism' and 'tyranny' will not do. It is something new which is in my mind. I must therefore try to describe it, because I cannot give it a name. . . . I can see an immense crowd of men, who resemble one another and who are all equal, all ceaselessly revolving in their tracks in order

to procure for themselves the small, vulgar pleasures which overwhelm their souls. Each of them, drawn apart a little, is as it were a stranger to the fate of all the others. His children and his own special friends are the whole human species for him . . . he exists in himself and for himself alone and, even if it can still be said that he has a family, at least it is certain that he no longer has a country.

Above all this crowd there rises an immense tutelary power which takes upon itself to assure their enjoyment and to watch over their destinies. It is absolute, minutely punc-tilious, orderly, foreseeing, and mild. It would resemble the power of a father if its object were, like that of a father, to prepare men for their maturity. But, on the contrary, its object is solely to ensure that the people should remain per-manently fixed in infancy. . . . It ensures their security, fore-sees and satisfies their needs, makes possible their pleasures, conducts their most serious business for them, oversees their industries. . . . Thus, every day it renders the use of free will less useful and less frequent. . . . Egalitarianism has prepared men for all these things: it has made them ready to suffer them, often, indeed, to regard them as a blessing. . . .

[The Sovereign Power] does not break wills, it softens them, it bends and guides them. . . . It is not tyrannous: it prevents, it constrains, it enervates, it dazes, it stupefies, and it reduces in the end each nation to no more than a flock of timid and hardworking beasts, whose government is their shepherd.

I have always believed that this kind of regulated, mild, and non-violent slavery which I have depicted could be combined much better than one might suppose with some of the exterior forms of liberty, and that it would not be impossible for it to set itself up even within the shadow of popular sovereignty.

Our contemporaries are driven incessantly by two incom-patible passions: they feel the need to be led, and the desire to remain free. . . . They therefore combine centralization with popular sovereignty. This provides them with some relief. They console themselves for being under tutelage with the thought that they chose their guardian themselves. Each individual accepts the fact that he is chained because he can see that it is not a man or a class, but the people itself which holds the end of the chain.

In this system, the citizens emerge for a moment from their state of dependence in order to choose their master, and then withdraw once more . . .

However, I would certainly not deny that the polity which I have described is infinitely preferable to what happens when, after all power has been centralized, it is then deposited in the hands of a man or body of men who are responsible to no one. Of all the forms which democratic despotism could take, this would beyond doubt be the worst.[39]

Allowing for a certain amount of fraud and force, 'democratic despotism' in the twentieth century has arisen in the latter manner. However, something approximating to de Tocqueville's argument about the first kind of mass democracy provides the basis for some of the criticism of totalitarianism as a valid concept. It is for this reason that the passage has been quoted at some length, since it is to the question of the validity and usefulness of the concept of totalitarianism as such that we must turn in the next and last chapter.

5/How Useful Is The Concept?

Vain search for a definition

If the arguments developed in the last chapter are sound, it would seem to follow that the three régimes to which the term 'totalitarian' became attached were régimes of a new type—indeed genuine 'prototypes', as they have been called throughout this essay. They were new not because none of the features which they exhibited had been observed before—indeed most of them had. But they were new because these features were exhibited within a framework of mass democracy; because their governments derived, or claimed to derive, their legitimacy from mass approbation, and used a democratic formula to describe their aims, at all events in part; and they were also different from comparable régimes that had gone before because they disposed of modern technological devices. Moreover, it would seem to be the case that the very concept of 'totalitarianism' is a new one, although once again many of its elements could be found in the ideas of political philosophers across the centuries. In the light of these conclusions it would seem that the adoption of a new term to describe the three régimes in the early 1930s was justifiable, and the use of the term as applied to these three societies proper and valid.

But a problem is raised by the fact that the term has been widely used, especially since the Second World War, for a very large number of societies of different structures and characters. To what extent has such usage been valid, and how is one to decide this question?

Again, there is one group of countries which presents little problem: this consists of those whose political régimes were modelled closely on that of the Soviet Union under Stalin to such an extent as to share their essential features. In this group fall the Soviet-dominated countries of Eastern and Central Europe, the 'People's

Democracies', so long as this domination continued in its original extent, that is, up to about 1956; China after the Communist victory of 1949; and Cuba since 1959. Although it seems legitimate to group these régimes together as totalitarian this is not to suggest that they are identical either in origin or in structure. Communist China modelled its government on that of the Soviet Union. But it had in the person of Mao an indigenous Leader, and both its ideology and its system of rule bear strong individual characteristics. Nevertheless it can hardly be disputed that the contours of totalitarianism, as sketched above, all apply to China. In the 'People's Democracies' which arose after the Second World War, with the exception of Yugoslavia both the Leaders and the systems were, in effect, imposed by Soviet military might, and to a large extent maintained in being by Soviet power. Once in being, however, their systems functioned in a manner so similar to that of the Soviet Union that the description 'totalitarian' is once again justified. The situation altered fundamentally when once the Soviet grip had been relaxed after Stalin's death; and the appropriateness of the continuing description of them as 'totalitarian' will therefore be discussed below.

Cuba, after the victory of Fidel Castro, is a different case again. Castro is essentially an indigenous Latin American *Caudillo*, or Leader, and it was only some time after he had come to power that he proclaimed himself a Marxist and began to use ideology in the accepted totalitarian manner. The method of rule in Cuba is, again, in many respects different from that of the Soviet Union. But Cuba under Castro displays all the characteristic features of the prototypes: the charismatic Leader, mass legitimacy, mass mobilization, the subjugation of the legal order, the subversion of the institutions of the state, the manipulated ideology. Cuba moreover claims to be the centre for the spread of revolution to the American continent. It can therefore rightly be called totalitarian.[1] In contrast, the rule of another Leader, that of Trujillo over the Dominican Republic, while as oppressive as that of Castro, cannot be so described, since it lacked both ideology and mass mobilization: it was a police state, and little more.[2]

Greater difficulty arises when considering the validity of the term 'totalitarian' as applied to a number of régimes in the decade before the Second World War, and after the war, to which the term 'Fascist' was applied, because of certain outward resemblances to the Italy of Mussolini—Japan, Argentina, Spain, or Portugal, for example. Similar difficulties arise with regard to Soviet Russia both before the advent of Stalin and since Stalin's death, to Communist countries since 1956, and to a number of new countries with one-party régimes and with governments based on dictatorship which have come into existence since the end of the Second World War. Are they or were they totalitarian? And how does one decide?

The search for a definition of 'totalitarianism' has proceeded unremittingly for twenty-five years or more. The literature on the subject is immense, and approaches vary in a bewildering way, according to the interest of the author. The sociologically inclined author will ask the question as to why it arises in one country and not in another, what are the social factors which lead one country but not another along the path of totalitarianism.[3] The psycho-logically inclined author will want to study the inner springs of man's motives which lead him to set up, or to tolerate, societies of this nature.[4] Such studies, while of immense interest and value, fall outside the scope of an enquiry into the nature of a concept. Many political scientists have searched more specifically for a definitive model which will enable one to classify states as 'totalitarian' or not, according as the model fits. The large number of such attempts makes the journey through the modern literature a hazardous one, though fortunately there are several reliable guides.[5] Even a cur-sory examination of the large collection of definitions which can now be assembled will reveal the extent to which every definition reflects the predilection of the author for what he believes to be the key to the real nature of the régime. The historical approach which has been attempted in the preceding chapters made definition un-necessary: what was needed was a description of the features of certain specific societies to which the term was actually applied when it came into the language. But if a touchstone is required for wider application the need for definition may arise, and which is one to select?

The present author's predilection has been made clear enough: it lies in the direction of the view which sees totalitarian rule as a form of personalized rule by a Leader and an élite who seek to dominate *both* society *and* the regular, legal structure which is called 'the state'. If I had to devise a definition its paternity would, I believe, be found in the views of four authors in particular: Hannah Arendt, Franz Neumann, Robert C. Tucker, and Hans Buchheim, who recognized, as so many have failed to recognize, that 'totalitarianism' is not in any sense a strong police dictatorship writ large, but is something different in kind, and does not partake of the essential quality of what for centuries in Europe has characterized the notion of the state.

Hannah Arendt's *Origins of Totalitarianism*, first published in 1951, is an imaginative and profound attempt to look at the emergence of the totalitarian régimes as a social and historical phenomenon of our generation. Among the many insights which the book contains three in particular stand out.

First is the recognition that totalitarian lawlessness is lawlessness of a particular, and novel, kind, since it is lawlessness masquerading as constitutionalism: the state machine, emasculated and manipulated by the party, nevertheless remains in being and on show. Miss Arendt was right to stress this difference, even if her emphasis on the rôle of the party was too great (in the light of what has been shown to have been the actual position in Chapter 3 above): it is not so much the party as the *apparat* which the Leader calls upon to exercise his lawless rule, and for shorter or longer periods the totalitarian Leader wages war against his party. But the *Origins of Totalitarianism* served to remind us that totalitarianism was not just another example of a powerful state such as Byzantium, or the Roman Republic under Julius Caesar. Second, Miss Arendt recognized that ideology in the totalitarian systems had little to do with ideas or beliefs, but was an instrument for manipulating the population, and thus helping to consolidate the ruling élite's hold over it. And thirdly, she discerned the special function which terror performs for the totalitarian Leader: this is not merely to frighten people into submission, but rather to isolate each individual, to leave him enclosed by a wall of loneliness, shut off from the support and comfort of his family, his friends and, of course, any kind of free association of his fellows.

This process, to which the name 'atomization' is sometimes given, is the one by means of which the Leader can, at the height of his power, break almost any spirit or crush moral resistance to his all-pervading 'ideology'. The notion of 'atomization' is not new, even if the word is—many writers, from Aristotle onwards, have emphasized how important it is for a tyrant to reduce individuals to moral loneliness or isolation by denying them the support of what Durkheim called 'intermediate societies'. In the three proto-types the isolation was, with the aid of modern technology, ex-tended and perfected to an extent that no former tyrant could ever have hoped to achieve—or, more accurately, this happened in two out of three of the prototypes, since Mussolini failed in his object. Isolation of the individual was brought about with the aid of the party which was used to penetrate and render harmless virtually all institutions of society. This remarkable device, invented by Lenin, has no complete counterpart in the history of mankind, and provides a further argument for the novelty of totalitarianism.

But dominant parties, which originate in revolutionary mass movements, are not confined to régimes which exhibit the features which are associated with totalitarianism. Robert C. Tucker made an important contribution to our understanding of the problem by recognizing that not all the dictatorships which emerged as the re-sult of the victory of such a 'revolutionary mass-movement régime under single-party auspices' can be classified as totalitarian. The distinguishing feature he recognized in the 'psychology, or more accurately the psychopathology, of the leader', which in the régime which becomes totalitarian (as distinct, say, from Tunisia, Turkey under Kemal Ataturk or China under the Kuomintang) results in the party which grows out of the movement being reduced by the Leader to a cog in the apparatus of rule. Tucker draws the con-trast in the history of the Soviet Union between the régime of Lenin and the régime of Stalin: in the former the party retains its existence as an independent institution, in the latter it is broken and reduced by the Leader to an instrument which he uses as part of his *apparat*. To these contrasting results of revolutionary régimes Tucker gives the names of 'Bolshevik' and 'führerist' types of régime respectively.[6]

Franz Neumann, in an essay which remained unfinished at his premature death in 1954, recognized the importance of distinguishing between absolutist régimes, however powerful, and the totalitarian dictatorships. It is not merely a question of more or less political power, he says: it is a qualitative, not a quantitative difference.

> Where, as in the absolute monarchy, power is primarily exercised through the traditional bureaucratic instruments of coercion, its operation is governed by abstract, calculable rules, although their execution often may be arbitrary. Absolutism, therefore, already contains the major institutional principles of modern liberalism. Totalitarian dictatorship, on the other hand, is the absolute negation of these principles, because the main repressive agencies are not courts and administrative bodies, but the secret police and the party.[7]

Hans Buchheim was, so far as I know, the first expressly to point out (in 1962) the danger of confusing totalitarianism with mere substantial increase of state power—though some notion of the distinction is inherent in the work of Arendt, Tucker, and Neumann already referred to. He wrote:

> It is a dangerous error to regard totalitarian rule as an excess of state power. In reality, both the state and political life properly understood are among the most important and fundamental factors for our protection against totalitarianism. . . . Genuine politicization of society and the unity of state and society are a part of democracy no less than they are of the total state. The characteristic feature of totalitarian rule is the subjugation of both state and society together under an utopian, non-political claim to exercise rule.[8]

It would be easy now to construct a definition of totalitarianism which would embody both the features which have been discussed in earlier chapters, and the interpretations which have been summarized in the preceding paragraphs. Yet such a definition would serve little purpose. It would, at best, reflect the view arrived at by one author on the nature of totalitarian rule, under the influence of earlier work which has led him to his conclusions. Other definitions could be constructed which would epitomize quite a different interpretation of the evidence. But to what purpose? Such definitions are merely shorthand formulae for one man's view of politics, and can have no claim to universality, let alone to objective validity in terms of truth or untruth. It is better to remain in the realm of fact: it is for this reason that the historical method has been adopted in this essay. Certain régimes with ascertainable features were in fact described in the English language as 'totalitarian' after 1928 or 1929: the evidence of history suggests that the new term did in fact correspond to a new concept and to a new form. In order to discover whether the term can properly be applied to some régime other than the three to which it was originally applied the proper course is to compare the features of that régime with those of the original three; and not to prejudge the enquiry by a definition which would necessarily be idiosyncratic in its nature.

Attacks on the concept

However, in recent years criticism has been levelled at the term 'totalitarianism' on the grounds that it is a misleading term, or at best out of date, that it is a politically loaded term used with improper motives, or that it confuses the study of political systems by designating a class of societies which does not in fact exist. At the risk of oversimplification, the attacks on the use of the term 'totalitarianism' can be summarized under three heads. First, that it is a 'cold war' term, of no scientific validity, coined in order to enable the United States to project on the world a clear black-and-white contrast between the United States as the champion and the symbol of freedom, and the Soviet Union and the other Communist countries as examples of slavery and aggression. This is the view propounded by Herbert J. Spiro, who argues that the features said to be characteristic of 'totalitarian' states, such as the intensive use of ideology, are not in fact peculiar to them, but are to be found in other types of polities, and that the term has been used, especially in the United States, in order 'to fashion an ideology for the "free world" ', and 'to marshal popular commitment to the new ideology'.[9]

In its extreme form (which is not propounded by Spiro) this view has been championed by Herbert Marcuse. His criticism of 'totalitarianism' as a valid concept is based on the contention that the restrictive and dictatorial features which are said to characterize, say, the Soviet Union are little different from those which characterize those states which are wrongly contrasted with the Soviet Union, such as the United States of America. The outward forms in the United States may be different—the several political parties, the variety of newspapers, the apparent freedom of speech and expression, the apparent absence, or relative absence, of constraint. But this seeming liberty 'under the rule of a repressive whole' becomes 'a powerful instrument of domination'. The range of choice open to the individual is not the decisive factor in determining the degree of human freedom, but '*what* can be chosen and what *is* chosen by the individual'. Like the so-called totalitarian societies, the modern advanced industrial society, even where it professes to be democratic in fact

> . . . tends to be totalitarian. For 'totalitarian' is not only a terroristic political co-ordination of society, but also a non-terroristic economic-technical co-ordination which operates through the manipulation of needs by vested interests. It thus precludes the emergence of an effective opposition against the whole. Not only a specific form of government or party rule makes for totalitarianism, but also a specific system of production and distribution which may well be compatible with a 'pluralism', of parties, newspapers, 'counter-vailing powers', etc.[10]

It is because this society will protect itself by suppressing actions calculated to destroy it that Marcuse subsequently advocated what he called 'liberating tolerance', in place of what he regards as the existing 'repressive tolerance' in the United States. This he says, 'would mean intolerance against movements from the

Right and toleration of movements from the Left'. The scope of this new form of tolerance 'would extend to the stage of action as well as of discussion and propaganda of deed as well as of word'.[11]

Marcuse thus turns the attack on a political term into a call for revolutionary action. But there is a second line of attack on this term which, like Spiro's and unlike Marcuse's, is based on political analysis and not on political passion. This line has developed as the result of the changes which have been taking place in the Soviet Union and in the Communist countries of Eastern and Central Europe since the death of Stalin in 1953, and has many champions, of whom Michael Curtis may be selected as the most moderate, reasonable, and convincing. Curtis starts with an analysis of the prototypes which recognizes the novel features which distinguished them from tyrannies of past ages—in particular, the insistence by the modern Leaders on mass participation and mass enthusiasm. But, he says, 'useful though the term has been' the time has come for a new concept which will take account of the changes which have taken place since Stalin's death; moreover, 'the concept of totalitarianism, if applied automatically to all the Communist countries, disregards not only the changing nature of the Soviet Union, but also the diversity of the different régimes in which changes have occurred at different rates'. In the light of these changes, to cling to the term merely obscures the process of political comparison by erecting an artificial mental barrier between a Communist society and a non-Communist one.[12] (One could add, though Curtis does not touch upon this in his argument, that to apply the term 'Fascist' to such different régimes as National Socialist Germany on the one hand and South Africa, Greece, Spain or some of the Latin American countries on the other, would have the effect of erecting an artificial mental barrier to political analysis, and obscure diversities by over-emphasizing outward similarities.)

The third line of attack, that of Benjamin R. Barber, derives from the view that the traditional analysis of a polity in terms of the relationship between those who rule and those who are ruled, treated as distinct and separate categories, is out of date and irrelevant in modern conditions.

> Totalitarianism [Barber says] has a generally accepted
> meaning only insofar as we focus on the totalistic element in
> it, conceived in narrow statist terms; statism, in turn, makes
> sense only if we pre-suppose, in the manner of traditional
> liberal theory, a dualistic cleavage between abstract public
> and private spheres. . . . In the present century, it has been
> generally acknowledged that power can be a function not
> simply of a formally defined public realm but also of social
> and economic forces that stalk, but are not part of the pri-
> vate realm, and that individuals can be victimized by
> 'private' monopolies beyond the pale of public regulation or
> control. Indeed, because the state is politically controllable
> and its activities are visible, its threats to personal liberty
> are, in some ways, less pernicious than those emanating
> from unrecognized influence—sources operating under
> assumed but totally unreal conditions of equality in a
> supposedly fragmented and pluralistic private sphere.[13]

Such, then, is the case against the retention of the term
'totalitarianism': it is a 'cold war' implement, which improperly
masks the essential similarity between the United States and the
Soviet Union; it was useful in the past, but has been overtaken by
changes in the Soviet Union and elsewhere; and it is based on the
outmoded notion that the individual's liberty is threatened by the
state, whereas in fact it is threatened by private elements within the
state which are outside public control. Allowing for a certain
partisan exaggeration, there is some force in all these arguments.

It is not true to say that the use of the term 'totalitarian' as
equally applicable to National Socialist Germany and the Soviet
Union under Stalin is subsequent to, or a consequence of, the 'Cold
War' (meaning, one presumes, the point at which the United States
and some Western European countries realized the expansionist
intentions of the Soviet Union), but there is no doubt that the free
(and inaccurate) use of the term increased enormously after the end
of the Second World War—especially by politicians.[14] Marcuse's
argument may be in effect a call to revolution rather than a rea-
soned statement of the case: it is, to say the least, unrealistic to

condemn any society for refusing to commit suicide by surrendering to forces which wish to destroy it, however much one may sympathize with the motives of the revolutionaries. It is, however, the case that a modern industrial mass democracy constrains and shapes the individual by means much more indirect than the usual organs of state repression—by mass persuasion, by the power of commercial advertising and by social pressure for conformity. It is no doubt also true that these new forms of restraint are quite compatible with a free press and with a multi-party system of electing a government, in view of the large measure of agreement on the basis of society shared by competing parties and newspapers. It will be recalled that the possibility of the development of a modern industrial democracy somewhat along these lines was foreseen by de Tocqueville in the passage which was quoted at the end of the last chapter.

Again, the changes which have taken place, since the death of Stalin, in the Soviet Union and in other Communist countries are certainly very considerable. In one Communist country, Yugoslavia, evolution has taken place towards what can now be described as a pluralist state, with considerable freedom of speech and with at least an incipient legal order. In the Soviet Union there is no longer an all-dominating Leader, which was the most important contour discernible under Stalin. There is a dissent movement which would have been inconceivable under Stalin. There is considerably increased contact with and knowledge of the world outside the Communist sphere. Scientific research has been liberated from a dogmatic strait-jacket.

It is even possible to discern some signs of pluralism in the shape of pressure by different interests on the government to promote their own ends.[15] Peter Ludz, in his study of the ruling élite of Eastern Germany, has shown a shift towards what he calls 'consultative authoritarianism': this is exemplified in a younger and more technically minded party Central Committee, greater mobility within the party apparatus for the technically trained and, so far as ideology is concerned, in a kind of institutionalized revisionism which is moving in the direction of greater rationality in decision making.[16] In all the People's Democracies trends towards some kind of pluralism can be discerned, at any rate to the extent that the different elements which compose the ruling *apparat* are in a state of rivalry and conflict, each with the aim of promoting its own interests.[17] Finally, it would be difficult to deny the threat which is posed to individual liberty in a modern industrial society by forces other than the state itself—trade unions, the great commercial enterprises and the many indirect pressures exercised on education, on employment and on the use of leisure.

However, it is the contention of this essay that none of these arguments is sufficient to render the term 'totalitarianism' invalid as a distinct and discrete description of something which both as a concept and in its practical manifestations remains different from other concepts and régimes. The fact that a term is abused by politicians for improper ends does not mean that it is necessarily invalid as a precise description when used within limits which are justified by strict analysis, and supported by reason and by evidence. To take a simple parallel, 'Fascism' has of late become a term of vulgar abuse in the mouths of demagogues for almost anything which they dislike. Yet, Fascism is a doctrine with a discernible history and definite meaning in twentieth-century Europe, and the language of politics would be the poorer if it were discarded. In the same way, 'totalitarianism', though abused, can be submitted to rigorous analysis in order to ascertain when it may, and when it should not be used. The case for rejecting it, therefore, cannot be based on the fact that it is frequently abused: rejection can only be justified, if at all, by one of the other three arguments which have been adduced against its retention.

The argument based on the similarity between two mass industrial societies such as, say, the United States and the Soviet Union, in spite of some superficial validity, will not stand up to examination. To be flippant for a moment—where is the equivalent of Marcuse, freely publishing and teaching in the USSR, and freely travelling beyond its confines? It is easy to accumulate a large number of criticisms of the United States, or any other non-Communist country for that matter, add them up and cry 'Identity!' The criticisms will, no doubt, in many cases be fully justified—they arise from the imperfections which are to be found in every liberal democratic system, and from the results which follow from the very nature of a vast, consumer-oriented mass democracy. But the argument for identity, or even close similarity (which is as far as Marcuse goes), breaks down when one considers those aspects of a liberal democratic society which, in his zeal to find a near-identity where none exists, the critic has ignored.

Thus, if it be the case that invisible pressures and interests foster an 'ideology' in the United States as all-pervasive as Soviet 'ideology' (which is not, in the opinion of this writer, true) it is also the case that in the United States no means exist to exclude other ideologies, or criticisms of the official one: such means exist in the Soviet Union. The citizen of the United States can appeal to the courts, which are by no means always ineffective in protecting the citizen—irrespective of his colour, for all that has been said to the contrary: the Soviet citizen, be he Baptist, or Crimean Tartar, or dissident intellectual will seek justice in the courts in vain, if once the machinery of the ruling élite has decided to turn against him. As recent years have demonstrated, the citizen of the United States has freely open to him all kinds of forms of protest, even in many cases of violent protest, with comparative immunity: the Soviet citizen has none. An American or group of Americans, denied in practice the rights and liberties to which the law entitles them can fight for these rights and liberties, with some measure of success, both in the courts and by democratic process. The changed status of black Americans over the past fifteen years (and whether or no the change is complete or adequate is immaterial to this argument), bears witness to the fact that neither courts nor protests are entirely ineffective in the United States. The Soviet citizen has no legal means of any kind to enforce the rights and liberties which his sham constitution pretends to guarantee. The courts are closed to him, since judicial review is not recognized in Soviet law; while if he resorts to any form of public protest he can be (and usually is) tried and sentenced on a criminal charge, such as slandering the Soviet Union, or the like. The past years have witnessed countless examples of this. Again, the citizen of the United States can emigrate, the Soviet citizen can not.

It is certainly true that economic restraints inhibit the freedom of the citizen of the United States to change his employment at will, or to accumulate sufficient wealth to provide him with independence. There are many cases where powerful business concerns can force destitution on thousands of share-holders or employees. But the freedom exists for some, and the degree of social mobility which exists in the country at any rate offers some hope to many millions of Americans that they will be the fortunate ones. Even this degree of hope is absent in the Soviet Union, where the ruling élite can, and frequently does, keep complete control over the employment of every citizen, and can render him destitute at will. The absence of private enterprise and restrictions on the accumulation and inheritance of property make economic independence an unattainable goal for all. These, and other, differences between the two countries are real and substantial. They are differences of kind, not of degree; and no amount of ingenious argument can make them disappear.

The argument based on the changes which have taken place in the Soviet Union and other Communist countries must also take account of these realities. It is certainly true as Curtis contends that much damage can be done to political enquiry by forcing into one category political systems which are really diverse in their features: but, if, in spite of diversity, there remain certain basic and distinct features, then those political systems which share them can properly be classed together.

The apparent absence in the Soviet Union and in other Communist countries of a Leader, in the sense that Stalin was the Leader, is the strongest single factor which goes to support Curtis's theory. However dominant the influence of Khrushchev and of Brezhnev may have been in Soviet politics after 1953, a number of significant differences seem to persist. The party has acquired something of the character of an independent institution, even if it it is still, as before, controlled from the top by its Secretariat, which in turn is controlled by its General Secretary. The emergence of 'collective leadership', means, in practice, that decisions are no longer imposed on the Politburo by one man who controls all the instruments of rule (party, police, state bureaucracy) but are the result of agreement between several powerful leaders—and especially the heads of the party and state apparatus. This, in turn, means that some kind of independence is becoming discernible in each apparatus, even rivalry between them. This rivalry between different divisions of the ruling *apparat*—party, state bureaucracy, police, army—is even more marked in the Communist countries of Eastern and Central Europe than it is as yet in the Soviet Union. It is clear that it could become incompatible with totalitarianism unless, as in National Socialist Germany, it is kept under full control by a Leader as dominant as Hitler. Mussolini completely failed to do this—hence his ultimate failure to erect his 'totalitarian state'. It is notable in this context that the downfall of Khrushchev in October 1964 was in part, at any rate, due to the fact that he attempted to gather once again all the threads of power into his own hands, and to assert the dominance of the party apparatus over the state apparatus and his own personal dominance over both.[18]

This is only one element of change. The second important element discernible—and more especially in some of the other Communist countries of Central and Eastern Europe—is the emergence of incipient 'pressure groups', such as the army, the party apparatus, the managers and possibly others. They are not real 'groups' in the sense that they have any independence or cohesion of their own. But the signs are multiplying that the pressure which they are beginning to exert on the government in order to promote their own view of policy or their own interests is not always without effect. Thirdly, there has grown up and persisted for a number of years inside the Soviet Union a vigorous movement of dissent—in the Orthodox Church and the other Christian denominations, among the Jews, among intellectuals including the scientists, and within some of the national minorities. Since totalitarianism depends for its survival, among other things, on the manipulated ideology, which in turns depends on full control over information and suppression of undesirable criticism, this new phenomenon is an important breach in the armour. Events in Czechoslovakia showed how rapidly internal dissent could lead to virtually complete eradication of the contours of the totalitarian régime such as the 'führerist' party, the Leader (Novotny), the subjugation of the law or the manipulated ideology. If the same should happen inside the USSR there would be no foreign army available, as there was in Czechoslovakia in 1968, to restore the outward crust of repression, while leaving the seething volcano underneath. Dissent is in many ways peculiar to the USSR. But elsewhere there are other comparable signs of the emergence of independent voices. In Poland, for example, the Catholic Church has survived as a separate and independent power, preaching unremittingly from some twelve thousand pulpits throughout the country a doctrine that is at the very least incompatible with the materialist foundations of Communism.

To what extent does all this amount to the erosion of totalitarianism in the Soviet Union and the countries of Eastern and Central Europe? Certain qualifications must be made. It is true that there is no Leader any more in the sense that Stalin was the Leader. Nevertheless the traditions of over twenty years of Stalin's supreme authority die hard; and the Soviet Union tends continuously towards a leadership system much in the same way as a man can feel pain in a limb which has been amputated. Khrushchev's attempt to make himself into a Leader failed: but already within five or six years of his fall there were signs that the new General Secretary was trying to assume that mantle of Leadership. Again, remarkable as the dissent movement may be, there is no sign as yet (January 1972) that it has reached the state where it can present a threat to the authority of the ruling élite. The parallel with Czechoslovakia (however deeply developments in that country may have alarmed the Soviet authorities), cannot be pushed too far: it will only become complete if and when critical voices begin to be raised within the Soviet Communist Party as they were in the Czech Communist Party, and not merely in intellectual and, to a lesser extent, scientific circles. The incipient 'pressure groups' have not, as yet, ever attempted to challenge the decision-making rôle of the Politburo. The manipulated ideology is dented, but far from broken. The law has made some attempts to assert its independence: it still remains subjugated to the will of the ruling élite. The exercise of arbitrary terror, though it still survives, cannot of course be compared in its extent to what went on under Stalin. But the virtual control over every man's livelihood which the ruling élite wields is quite adequate to enforce compliance in the case of all but the most courageous, for whom the rigged and pre-judged trial or the certification in lunacy by the venal psychiatrists of the security forces has to be invoked.

Thus, when all allowance has been made for the real changes that have taken place in the USSR since 1953—the decline of the Leader, the reduction of terror, the revival of the party as an institution and, at all events for a period, the differentiation of party and government apparatuses in regard to the functions which they perform, the emergence of dissent, the decline of ideology as an effective controlling device, the persistent survival and revival of religion, the first signs of something approximating to group interests exercising pressure on the ruling élite—one thing nevertheless persists which is characteristic of the totalitarian régime. This is the complete lack of that differentiation and distinctiveness of areas of power and responsibility which, it has been argued above, is the necessary feature of the 'state' as traditionally developed in the political concepts of European political thought. The 'state', in this sense, argues a complex of interlocking and interdependent institutions; yet each has its distinct right and functions, and each can, within the prescribed limits, preserve the independence which goes with its functions.

Over all and above all, the distinct and independent legal order provides the practical means by which each institution preserves this independence—either by recourse to the judicial machinery, or by virtue of a well-established practice of political behaviour which it is very difficult for any person or group of persons to breach. To take two simple and homely examples from England of the way in which the legal order protects from excessive encroachment on the life of the individual. Wrongful arrest or other oppressive actions by the executive can normally be put right by appeal to the courts, or at all events by a subsequent action for redress. The fact that there are cases where such redress is not available in the courts does not invalidate the contention: it merely gives rise to a case for reform. Moreover, a whole array of independent bodies— trade unions, professional bodies, private societies, newspapers— is available to bring pressure for redress on the executive, and each can act with perfect safety to itself. Oppressive action by the legislature—apart from the sanction of the forthcoming election—is, to quite a considerable extent, inhibited by the force of public opinion. To take an example. The Standing Orders of the House of Commons do not, of themselves, make it impossible for the party with a majority in the House to silence the opposition: it is difficult to conceive, in normal circumstances, that this could happen. At the root of this state of affairs lies the large degree of distinctiveness and independence and fixed limits of competence of the different institutions which make up the British polity—the executive, the legislature, the judiciary, free public opinion and the host of other minor institutions of public life, down to the individual corporation and person.

It is these features of distinctiveness, independence and fixed limits of competence which are completely absent in the USSR, in spite of all the changes which have taken place; and it is this absence which entitles one to speak of the ruling power in the Soviet Union as an *apparat*, lacking the qualities associated with the 'state'— which it was argued above is the distinctive characteristic of the totalitarian régime. An admirable illustration of this lack of independence and distinctiveness of institutions is provided by an account published in 1971 of the forcible detention in a lunatic asylum of a scientist, Zhores Medvedev, whose critical writings had offended 'the authorities'—it is characteristic of this Kafka-like world of totalitarianism that it never became clear to the victim and those near to him who the particular 'authority' was that set in motion the detention which, even in terms of the vague provisions of the Soviet law on the subject, was illegal—the KGB, the local Soviet, or the local party, or some indeterminate 'higher up'. In fact, this uncertainty as to the origin of an instruction or a policy is characteristic of the *apparat* in action: behind the façade of the nominally and ostensibly distinct institutions, the real ruling power operates through whatever instruments it finds most convenient.

Dr Medvedev could neither recover his liberty through the courts, nor seek redress by action after the event, since neither remedy is provided for in Soviet law. In this particular case each of the separate 'authorities' at the local level to which appeals were made by the brother, wife, and influential friends of the detained man was evasive, incapable of action, and covered up its own servile incompetence by lying and trickery—the KGB, the Ministry of Health, the medical bodies, the party, and the local Soviet. Release was obtained as a result of over two weeks of agitation and pressure by courageous individuals, both inside and outside the USSR, and at all levels. Nor was this release the result of intervention from a higher level to put right an error at a lower level. On the contrary, the release was due precisely to the fear that the publicity which the case was arousing outside the USSR would reflect, not on individual incompetent or dishonest psychiatrists, not on individual officials who had exceeded their authority, but on the central ruling *apparat* itself, from whom in some form the order to start the whole process had emanated. Moreover, the action which eventually succeeded was exclusively the action of courageous individuals: the medical profession as a whole, or the official representative bodies of scientists, being as they are subordinate to the control of the party, were quite unwilling to do anything in the matter, and displayed no corporate spirit or professional ethic whatever.[19]

In microcosm this case contains within it the quintessence of totalitarian rule: the superior power which can override all ostensible institutions; the subjugation of the legal order; the lack of discrete and separate organs of power—in short the omnipresence of *total* control over the individual. But it also illustrates the extent to which totalitarian rule depends for its success on secrecy, isolation from the outside world, and successful deception of the outside world. The fact that the 'iron curtain' has now been breached to the extent that news which the Soviet authorities wish to conceal can nevertheless reach the foreign press and, in the case of writers and scientists, foreign colleagues, was decisive in this case. For there can be no doubt that if the Soviet authorities could have prevented news of Medvedev's detention in the asylum from reaching the outside world, and could have put out their own distorted prevarications on the case without fear of contradiction, he would still be under forcible narcotic treatment in a ward for dangerous lunatics in the Kaluga mental hospital.

Nevertheless, it is difficult to draw a line of identity between Stalin's Russia and that of today, and to give the political systems operating in the two the same unqualified classificatory name, 'totalitarianism'. The most that can with accuracy be said about the Soviet Union and the other Communist countries is that they are at the present time (1972) in a state of transition, still recovering from the demise of the supreme Leader. Only time will show whether the transition stage will lead back to something closer to the original form of totalitarianism; or away from it to some less easily definable system of dictatorship, of which the world offers innumerable examples. There is therefore much force in the contention of Curtis, and of those who think like him, but it is nevertheless still too early to say that they are right; and events may prove them wroug.

Finally, there is the argument advanced by Barber, that the ruler-ruled dichotomy is out of date because it fails to take account of influences operating within the private sectors of society which escape the ruler's control. This argument may or may not be valid as an aspect of criticism of the United States: it is of no help in understanding the USSR. For the essence of Soviet government still remains the persistence of powerful bodies within the ostensibly 'private' sector, which are in fact controlled and used by the ruling élite, with the aid of the party. Such are the Soviet Writers' Union, the other cultural and scientific unions, the universities, the legal and medical professional bodies and the like. There is virtually no 'private' sector in the Soviet Union. For the Soviet citizen the ruler-ruled relationship is therefore the only one which retains any meaning or validity in determining his life, his liberty, and his scope of action. To ignore this fact is to deprive ourselves of the only criterion which we have for determining the nature of the Soviet political system.

By way of a conclusion

To sum up. Totalitarianism is a new form of dictatorship which grew up in the conditions of mass democracy after the First World War. It was characterized by the predominance of the

Leader of the victorious movement, who, with the aid of his subordinate élite and a manipulated ideology, aimed at total control over state, society and the individual. Leader and élite, by claiming the right to interpret the official ideology, in effect embodied both church and state: they subverted the law to their own ends and claimed to control private morality. They mobilized mass enthusiasm and support, from which they claimed to derive their legitimacy. In National Socialist Germany and in Stalin's Russia these aims were achieved as nearly, perhaps, as it is ever possible to achieve them, since man's resistance to tyranny is never easily quenched. In Mussolini's Italy the aims remained to a much greater extent in the realms of rhetoric. The survival of the monarchy and of the Catholic Church and Mussolini's inability in practice to break the resistance and independence of powerful institutions such as the police and the army all served to render much of the so-called 'totalitarian state' which he invented a ramshackle sham. The concept on which these three régimes were based was nevertheless a new one. The failure of Mussolini merely served to underline the features which were essential to justify the application of the new term; and to emphasize the obvious fact that in a society based primarily on leadership the ultimate, determining factor will always be the personality of the Leader.

But can there be any sure touchstone by which the survival of totalitarianism in any particular society can be determined? China would seem to offer a sufficient parallel to justify the use of the term, and especially since the decisive rôle of the Leader in his struggle against his party was illustrated in the Cultural Revolution. Cuba also seems to exhibit all the features which together make up the new type of régime. There are, no doubt, other cases —some of the 'People's Democracies', perhaps, such as Albania or Bulgaria where there has been little evolution since Stalin's day. In the case of the Soviet Union, it may be that we have to be content to note that it is at present in a state of transition, either back to totalitarianism or away from it, waiting, perhaps, for a new Leader of Stalin's calibre; or drifting towards a different form of oligarchic dictatorship, in which some of the features of totalitarianism will no longer survive. A rapid tour of some types of dictatorships which the world offers for our study today tends to support the view that there are many varieties of forms of dictatorship by one man, or by a self-perpetuating élite, in which some, but by no means all, the characteristic features of totalitarianism can be found. The best attempt that I know to provide some system of classification for this rich spectrum of political systems is that of Professor S. E. Finer:[20] all varieties exhibit some totalitarian features, yet none provides complete identity with the prototypes which must still remain the starting point of our enquiry, since it is they alone which can give a valid and ascertainable meaning to the term.

In his *Comparative Government* Finer, after dealing with the liberal-democratic and the totalitarian forms of government, proceeds to examine the various forms of autocracy and oligarchy which are to be found in the world today—indeed make up the majority of independent states. They fall, according to him, under three types: the Façade-Democracy, the Quasi-Democracy, and the Military Régime (the latter can exhibit a number of variants).

In the façade-democracy liberal-democratic institutions exist by law, with, in theory, appropriate safeguards: in practice the country is ruled by a traditional, established oligarchy consisting of a family, a group of families or a closed and privileged class. The essence of the method of rule is manipulation of the popular vote in order to keep the ruling élite in power. The legal right to vote is restricted by intimidation, discrimination or by falsification of the results. This procedure necessarily affects the exercise of the freedoms ostensibly guaranteed by the law or the constitution: but this restriction of freedom is in no sense ideological or doctrinal, it is merely designed for the end of more effective electoral manipulation. This form of façade-democracy survived until the 1920s in most of the Latin American countries, in the Balkan states, and in Iraq, Egypt and Iran in the Middle East. But the system was unable to adjust to changing social structure, such as the growth of towns and the rise of new social classes, and in particular to the growth of nationalism and an urge to 'modernize' among the military officers. In most cases the façade-democracies have undergone transformation to one of the other two forms, following upon the overthrow of the traditional ruling oligarchy. In some few cases, such as Chile and Uruguay, a form of liberal democracy emerged —in both countries at the time of writing (January 1972) the system is embattled and its survival precarious. The façade-democracies which still remain are all monarchies, with power mainly in the hands of one family and its supporters, and with rule exercised from the palace. Such are, for example, Iran, Jordan, and Morocco. The façade-democracy has in common with the totalitarian régimes manipulation of an ostensibly democratic electoral framework, and of the legal system: there the similarity ends. There is no ideology, no movement or party, no mobilization, no Leader, no grandiose aims of total control or of shaping a 'new man'.

With Finer's second category of 'quasi-democracy' we move a good deal nearer to totalitarianism. States in this category are characterized by a dominant party, which has usually emerged out of a victorious movement, and which either restricts the formation of other parties, or takes steps to ensure that such other parties as are permitted remain ineffectual. Mexico, after the revolution of 1911, is the sole example (apart from Turkey for a time) of the quasi-democracy outside Africa. In Africa this type of government was inaugurated when Tunisia became independent in 1956. There are now some dozen other examples.

The quasi-democracy, like the totalitarian régime, usually places restrictions on freedom of speech, press, person and domicile, and also usually limits the freedom of professional and social organizations to those which are controlled by the leading party. But the parties in the quasi-democracies do not normally have the cohesion or discipline of the party in the totalitarian régimes, nor do their leaders normally have the human and material resources or the will and drive, which are all necessary to achieve a totalitarian form of rule. However, the variety among the quasi-democracies in the world today is considerable. Thus, Mexico has probably been the most liberal and tolerant in practice, with a government record of stability and a system of rule which, if extensively based on patronage and corruption, nevertheless to a considerable degree reflects different interests and the main trends of public opinion. There is no ideology, and little party discipline. Tunisia is an example of one-man rule, in the sense that the country (which has only four million population) is run by Habib Bourguiba who is both head of the Néo-Destour ruling party and head of state. There is no official ideology; the Muslim religion, the family, private industry, trade, and agriculture all remain outside the party. Bourguiba's personal dictatorship, though capable of abuse, is in practice exercised with moderation. The police are powerful, but not all-powerful; imprisonment without trial exists, but is seldom used. Anyone can be arrested, but relatively few are. To some extent, as in Mexico, the party acts as an arbitrator or broker between competing pressure groups.

Tunisia is thus pragmatic, practical and undogmatic. It has little kinship, in spite of some similar features, with totalitarianism. Yet, how easily such a 'movement régime' can embark on the road to totalitarianism, given the desire to do so by its leader, is shown by the example of Ghana, until the overthrow of Kwame Nkrumah in 1966. His measures to sweep away every vestige of opposition and make himself undisputed sole ruler began immediately after Ghana achieved independence in 1957. Civil liberties were swept aside, a Nkrumah cult was instituted, arbitrariness abounded, the legislature, and eventually the courts, were packed. In imitation of abler adventurers before him, Nkrumah even devised an official ideology, 'Conscienscism'. There were treason trials and fake referenda. But the experience of Nkrumah proved very similar to that of Mussolini: like Mussolini, he was to learn to his cost that it is not enough to posture, to bully, to terrorize, and befuddle. Like Mussolini, and unlike Hitler or Stalin, Nkrumah failed to ensure that he effectively controlled through his party, the Convention People's Party, the civil service, the police and the armed forces. Like Mussolini, he was easily overthrown by the army and the police, and virtually no one rallied to his side, thus proving the lying and the play-acting behind all the ideology, the enthusiasm and the cult of the unhappy Osagefyo. Totalitarianism has to be more than play-acting to survive: though even play-acting can, it would seem, keep it going for some years.

The military régime can take many forms. Its emergence on the scene in so many of the countries of the world in recent times is determined by various factors—the social culture of the country concerned, the degree of the political maturity, the capacity of the military to intervene and the like. Military régimes can try to entrench themselves in permanent power, or can genuinely try to prepare the way for a return of civilian government; the extent to which they restrict civil liberties or permit, or rig, elections varies from case to case. The military may be found ruling directly, with more or less reliance on civilian elements, as in Greece, Nigeria, Pakistan, or Egypt; or they may, as in Spain or South Korea, merely act as one of two sources of support for the state—the Catholic Church and other civilian institutions in Spain, the parliamentary majority and a referendum in South Korea being examples of such a second source of support for a military dictatorship. Again, this has nothing to do with totalitarianism, as the example of Spain shows. For a short time General Franco found it expedient to use the trappings of Fascist doctrine and the support of the Falange. Once established in power, much of the doctrine was abandoned, and the Falange subjected to Franco's control and deprived of its political influence.[21] Spain emerged as an old-fashioned police state, with little regard for civil liberties, with an openly rigged parliament and wide-spread corruption. There is little mobilization of enthusiasm, virtually no official ideology—beyond that propagated by the Church—and no Utopian or millenary aims.

This rapid survey of Finer's illuminating classification of the varieties of arbitrary and dictatorial forms of government (other than the totalitarian ones) clearly illustrates how much the form of rule which develops in any particular state derives from traditions, social conditions, external factors, and its history.[22] But it shows above all, particularly in the examples of Bourguiba, Franco, and Nkrumah, how much the question whether evolution will take place in the totalitarian direction depends on the will and the personality of the dictator, or Leader of the movement. This confirms the conclusion arrived at in Chapter 2, that of all the contours or features of the three original totalitarian polities the most important and significant is that of the Leader. It is on his will, his character, his fanaticism, his ability to exploit social factors and traditions and his skill and determination in forcing his view of society on a credulous, cowed or emotionally disturbed population, that the emergence of totalitarianism will depend.

What, then, is the value of 'totalitarianism' as a concept? The evidence that has been adduced suggests that it stands for a distinct and new form of government which first became possible in the age of mass democracy, of modern technology and of twentieth-century nationalism. It can vary in its extent, in its success, in its totality—from the relative failure to erect a system of total power in the cases of Mussolini and Nkrumah, to the relative success of Hitler and Stalin. It is not a fixed and immutable form: it can change and evolve, as well as end in collapse and overthrow. It can develop into something approximating to liberal democracy, as in Yugoslavia or in the short-lived attempt in Czechoslovakia, which required brute force to put it down. It can co-exist, at all events for a time, with an independent church, as in Poland; with pluralism of institutions, as in some of the other Communist governments in the Central and East European 'People's Democracies'; and with dissent, incipient pressure groups and some pluralism of institutions in the Soviet Union. These instances of co-existence may well be transitional stages towards a different form of dictatorship, towards some kind of liberal democracy, or towards a return of full and unqualified totalitarian power. All this suggests that totalitarianism is not a final and immutable 'model' of government, but more in the nature of a spectrum, with varying degrees of intensity and totality.[23] But, just as on the spectrum one colour shades into the next, yet at certain points one distinct colour is clearly discernible, so there comes a point where a totalitarian régime is clearly discernible, even though this or that feature associated with it is absent or weak.

Perhaps as a concept totalitarianism is elusive, hard to define, liable to abuse by the demagogue, and, if wrongly used, a source of confusion when we are trying to find our way through the maze of the many forms which a polity can assume. Yet, we should be poorer without it, if only because we should lack the reminder that there are stages in the history of nations, perhaps of every nation, when the fanaticism, the arrogance, the ruthlessness, the ambition and the hubris of one individual can plunge millions of men and women into madness, suffering, fear and destruction.

London School of Economics and Political Science.

January 10, 1972

Notes and References

The names of authors to whom I refer or from whom I quote are in italics. Titles of their works will be found in the Bibliograpny. Where the Bibliography lists more than one work by a single author, the date of the relevant work follows the author's name in these Notes.

1/Introduction

1 *Opera*, Vol. XXI, p. 362.
2 *Gentile*, 1925, p. 39: 'Ma il fascismo . . . prima di tutto è una conuzione totale della vita.'
3 See an article in *Rinascita Liberale* of January 5, 1925 which refers to the (rigged) elections of April 1924 as 'totalitarie e liberticide', quoted in *De Felice*, p. 728.
4 *Opera*, Vol. XXXIV, pp. vi, 117–31.
5 See quotation in *Fraenkel*, pp. 59–60.
6 I am indebted for this suggestion and for some of the references to Dr Meir Michaelis.
7 'The Philosophical Basis of Fascism', *Foreign Affairs*, Vol. VI, No. 2, 1928.
8 For references to some of these descriptions see *Barber*, 1969, pp. 6–7.
9 *Marcuse*, 1968, p. 105.
10 *Fleron*, 1968, pp. 1–33.
11 A recent and important examination of the concept of totalitarianism Martin Jänicke's *Totalitäre Herrsshaft. Anatomie eines politischen Begriffes*, Berlin, 1971, was unfortunately not available to me when I wrote this study.

2/Contours and Features of Totalitarianism

1 *Friedrich*, 1954.
2 *Friedrich and Brzezinski*. This work was first published in 1956; the second edition, revised by Friedrich, appeared in 1965.
3 *Friedrich*, 1969, p. 126.
4 The contour on a map is what enables the experienced map-reader to recognize the distinctive characteristics of the countryside.
5 *Weber*, Vol. I, p. 179.
6 *Schapiro*, 1970, p. 299.
7 On Lenin generally see below, pp. 59–60.
8 For the text see *Aquarone*, pp. 581–90.
9 *Mack Smith*, p. 392; *Aquarone*, pp. 187–8.
10 See *Orlow*, *passim*.
11 The question of the rôle of the party in the three countries is discussed in more detail in the next chapter.
12 Quoted in *Aquarone*, p. 302, from the record of his conversations with Mussolini published by Ottavio Diude in 1953.
13 On this question see *Buchheim*, 1962 and *Buchheim*, 1968; see also *Diel-Thiele*, which confirms much of Buchheim's analysis on the basis of further research in the documents. The work of Buchheim offers, in general, the most penetrating analysis of totalitarianism that I have encountered. (His *TotalitäreHerrschaft* has also been translated into English.)

128/Notes and References

14 See *Picker*, pp. 201, 204, 222. The king did, indeed, formally remain head of state: those who lightly dismiss the institution of constitutional monarchy would do well to ponder the rôle which this fact played in the downfall of Mussolini and in the revival of liberty in Italy. Hitler had no such rival.

15 See, for example, K. Popov, 'Partiia i rol' vozhdia', *Partiinoe stroitel'stvo*, No. 1, 1930, pp. 3–9.

16 *Carlyle*, p. 415.

17 See his 'On the Relationship of Theory and Practice in Morality in General', reprinted in *Reiss*, at p. 74.

18 See under *Jellinek* and *Kelsen* in the bibliography.

19 *Buchheim*, 1968, p. 132.

20 Ibid., p. 130. The first to analyse this peculiarity of the Nazi system was Professor Ernst Fraenkel in *The Dual State*, published in the USA in 1941. The dualism, according to Fraenkel, is that of the 'Prerogative State' and the 'Normative State'. The use of the term 'state', at all events for the 'Prerogative' side, is unfortunate: the 'prerogative', or arbitrary power of the Leader is in fact directed against the 'Normative State'—as will be shown below.

21 *Aquarone*, pp. 235–46.

22 Quoted in *Buchheim*, 1968, pp. 196–7.

23 See *Lenin*, Vol. 31, pp. 291–2.

24 *Hart*, p. 58.

25 The validity of the parallel is discussed in Chapter 4.

26 This is a not untypical example of Gentile's involved and confused thinking. This quotation comes from the apologia for his career, written in 1943, after the collapse of the régime—see *Gentile*, 1960, p. 179. Gentile, who spent his last years in Florence, was murdered in 1946 by Communists—a further illustration of the close kinship of political morality which existed between the two extreme enemies of liberty in Italy.

27 In a speech in May 1925, quoted in *Harris*, p. 172.

28 See *Grossmann* for an account of the lesser known acts of resistance to National Socialism. For a summary of political, religious, and military resistance see *Bracher*, 1970, Chapter VII.

29 *Aquarone*, p. 293.

30 Quoted in *Binchy*, pp. 330–1.

31 *Bracher*, 1970, *loc. cit.*

32 For the best historical account see *Kolarz*. For the events of the decade after 1960 see two documentary collections—*Bourdeaux* 1968 and *Bourdeaux* 1969.

33 *Politics*, Book v, Chapter xi, Paras: 4–10.

34 See e.g. *Drath*.

35 See *Mason*.

36 See *Neumann* 1963, pp. 587–624 for the controls which were imposed after the outbreak of war.

37 Quoted in *Mack Smith*, p. 397.

38 *Fijalkowski*, pp. 208–10.

3/The Pillars of Totalitarianism

1 See *Pareto*, intro. pp. 33–51 by S. E. Finer, for a good guide and introduction to Pareto's theory of ideology.

2 Marx's views on this subject are to be found mainly in his *German Ideology* and in the *Communist Manifesto*. The whole question of the treatment of

ideology by Marx, Lenin, Kautsky and others is analysed in greater detail than before, to my knowledge, in a forthcoming book by Martin Seliger, *Ideology and Politics*, Chapter II, which I have enjoyed the advantage of using in manuscript.

3 *Pareto*, pp. 46, 84–5, 245–6.

4 My quotations are from the Russian text. An English translation of *What is to be Done?* will be found in Volume Five of the English edition of Lenin's *Collected Works*, at pp. 347–529.

5 *Opera* Vol. XXIV, pp. vi, 117–31.

6 This oft-repeated, and not undeserved, jibe against Italian Fascism was in fact put ironically into the mouths of his enemies by Mussolini himself in his speech of January 3, 1925 which accompanied his assumption of sole power: 'If fascism has been nothing more than castor oil and the *manganello* and not a proud emotion of the best elements of Italian youth, then the fault is mine!' Quoted in *De Felice* 1966, p. 721.

7 *Mack Smith*, pp. 410–17.

8 In his article in *Foreign Affairs* referred to in Chapter 1, footnote 7.

9 Franz Schurmann has suggested the division of ideologies into those which represent 'the manner of thinking of a class or an individual' and 'organizational ideologies', which he defines as 'a systematic set of ideas with active consequences serving the purpose of creating and using organization'—see *Schurmann*, p. 18. I prefer 'manipulated', since it seems to stress better the new elements which Lenin contributed to the concept.

10 The whole of this fascinating story is told in detail in *Wittfogel*, Chapter 9.

11 *The Origin of Civil Society*, Part VI, Section 5.

12 *Bracher*, 1970, Chapter IV; *Bullock*, p. 265.

13 For a detailed analysis of this story see *Schapiro*, 1955.

14 See *Fainsod*, 1963, pp. 323–7; *Armstrong*, pp. 134–5; *Fainsod*, 1958, pp. 85–6 and references under Rumyantsev; *Schapiro and Lewis*.

15 See *Nicolaevsky*, Section One.

16 See *Bullock*, p. 312.

17 For good summaries of Mussolini's rule see *Mack Smith*, Chapter 47, and *Aquarone, passim*.

18 *Chi'en Tuan-Sheng*, p. 149.

19 *Figgis*, p. 752.

19a It is not, presumably, accidental that the etymology of the Western European words 'state', 'état', 'Staat', 'stato' and 'estado' (all derived from the Latin 'status'), is connected with notions of ranking, order or establishment. In contrast, the only equivalent in Russian for 'state' is 'gosudarstvo', which means literally 'lordship' or 'Herrschaft'. Obviously, 'lordship' was a much more accurate description of the political system in Russia, at any rate up until 1906; and is much more apt than 'state' to describe the contemporary system.

20 *Diehl-Thiele*, p. 30.

21 Ibid., p. 31, footnote 85.

22 *Buchheim*, 1968, p. 157.

23 Ibid., p. 163.

24 Ibid., p. 197.

25 Ibid., pp. 215–41.

26 *Mack Smith*, pp. 394–7.

4/How New Is Totalitarianism?

1 For a fuller examination of the relationship of the views of Lenin and Tkachev see *Schapiro*, 1967, pp. 139–42.

2   The question of Lenin and Kautsky is fully discussed in the forthcoming book by Seliger, referred to in Chapter 3, footnote 2.

3   At the end of 1923—see *De Felice*, 1966, p. 465 note.

4   *Calvin*, Book IV, Chapter XX, SS 8 and 29. In practice, the Company of Pastors did act as a moral check on the civil government, and 'to remind Geneva's rulers to heed their responsibilities more carefully than they sometimes did'—see *Monter*, p. 144 and Chapter 6, *passim*.

5   The passages quoted are taken from an abridged translation of the *Six Books* by M. J. Tooley, Oxford (1955).

6   The following extract from Section 2 of the National Socialist Code of Criminal Law illustrates the extent to which the law was rendered totally ineffective as a means of protection available to the individual: 'Any one who commits an action which the law declares to be liable to a penalty shall be punished, as shall also anyone who deserves punishment in accordance with the principles underlying a penal law, as well as anyone who deserves punishment according to the sound and healthy instincts of the *Volk*. If there should be no definite criminal law enactment applicable to the action in question, then the action in question shall be punished in accordance with that law of which the basic principle seems most appropriate in the circumstances.' Quoted in *Staff*, p. 62. This work is invaluable on the whole subject of the National Socialist attitude to law.

7   From the eighth 'Letter from the Mountain', written in 1763.

8   I have used the translation by Maurice Cranston, published in Penguin Books in 1968.

9   *Constant*, p. 1049 *note* (my translation). See also Professor Cranston's Introduction to his translation of the *Social Contract*. The opposite case is presented in *Talmon*, 1952.

10 For a full discussion of the relationship of the philosophy of Hegel to totalitarian trends in European thought see *Popper*, Vol. II, Chapters 11 and 12.

11 The quotations are from the translation by T. M. Knox, Oxford, 1942. See also ibid. pp. 158–60, note, for Hegel's long diatribe against Carl Ludwig von Haller, the Swiss political philosopher (1768–1854) who argued that the principle that Might is Right was an unalienable, divine, just and desirable law of human society. The extent of Gentile's debt to the exaltation of the state in the *Philosophy of Right* is clearly evident: see *Gentile*, 1960, and numerous quotations from his works in *Harris*.

12 The most illuminating discussion of Marx's view of the state that I know is in *Avineri*, to which I am much beholden.

13 See especially 'On Co-operation' and 'On our revolution', both written in 1923.

14 See *Mosse* for a discussion of these influences on the young Hitler.

15 *Talmon*, 1952, pp. 6–8.

16 See *Schapiro*, 1955, p. 133, and reference there cited.

17 For a magnificent study of this literature see *Lichtenberger*.

18 See the Preface by the editor of the Soviet edition of 1947 reprinted in the French edition of the *Code* in the series 'Les Classiques du Peuple', Paris 1953.

19 See the Preface by Gilbert Chinard to his edition of Morelly's *Code de la Nature*, Paris 1950.

20 'I add this sketch of the laws in the form of an appendix . . . because unhappily it is all too true that it would be quite impossible in our day to create a republic of this type.' These are the words with which Morelly introduces the Fourth Part of his *Code*.

21 *Oeuvres*, Vol. xx, pp. 63–4; *Durkheim*, p. 196.
22 Ibid., Vol. xix, pp. 74, 82, 96 ('l'Industrie').
23 Ibid., Vol. xv, p. 58 (Postscript to 'Lettres d'un Habitant de Geneve').
24 Ibid., Vol. xx, pp. 50–61 ('L'Organisateur').
25 Ibid., Vol. xix, p. 158.
26 Chapter xi, sections 4–10. Sir Ernest Barker's translation.
27 *Andrewes*, pp. 73–4.
28 *Jones*, Chapters iv to ix; *Ehrenberg*, Chapter ii.
29 On tyranny in the classical world see *Andrewes, passim.*
30 *Wittfogel*, p. 92.
31 *Murra*, pp. 339–53.
32 *Wittfogel*, p. 249.
33 *Hussey*, Chapters xx, xxi and xxiii.
34 See *Oeuvres complètes de l'Abbé de Mably*, Lyon, 1796, Vol. ix, pp. 125–6;
    Monter, Chapters 4, 5, and 6; *Barrington Moore*, 19, pp. 30–88.
35 *Wittfogel*, p. 27.
36 Ibid., pp. 47–9.
37 Ibid., pp. 78, 87.
38 Ibid., Chapters 4 and 5, where the questions touched on here are fully
    discussed, with evidence in support.
39 *Tocqueville*, Vol. ii, Part 4, Chapter vi. The translation is my own. For a
    modern Utopia, somewhat on the lines of de Tocqueville's benevolent
    despotism, see *Skinner.*

5/How Useful Is the Concept?

1   See *Suarez, Kandt,* and *Cuba and the Rule of Law.*
2   See *Galindez.*
3   Among notable studies are *Barrington Moore, Kornhauser, Ludz,* 1964, and
    Arendt.
4   Among notable studies are *Cohn, Lifton, Oakeshott, Adorno,* and *Arendt.*
5   See e.g. *Barber,* 1965; and *Burrowes.*
6   See *Tucker,* Chapter i, and *Schapiro and Lewis* for further discussion of this
    classification, including the case of China.
7   *Neumann,* 1964, Chapter 9.
8   *Buchheim,* 1962, pp. 118–22. An English translation of this book has been
    published recently.
9   See his article 'Totalitarianism' in the *Encyclopaedia of the Social Sciences,*
    Vol. xvi, 1968.
10 *Marcuse,* 1968, p. 20, and *passim.*
11 *Marcuse,* 1969, pp. 122–3.
12 See *Curtis, passim.*
13 See *Barber,* pp. 33–4.
14 For the historical development of the term see pp. 12–13 above. Apart from
    Sabine and *The Times* the term 'totalitarian' was applied to Russia, Germany
    and Italy in the 1930s by other authors, such as Carleton Hayes—long be-
    fore the 'cold war' was thought of.
15 This question has now been closely studied in *Skilling and Griffiths.*
16 This is the conclusion which emerges from the vast material assembled in
    Ludz, 1968.
17 This is the main thesis developed in *Ionescu.*
18 On the emergence of competing segments of the ruling apparatus in the
    Soviet Union see *Schapiro,* 1970, 'Epilogue'.

19 See *Medvedev, passim.* Many more cases are known of the certification of dissentics as lunatics, but none other is known in such detail.

20 *Finer,* Chapters 9, 10, and 11. As those who have followed the argument of the first four chapters of this essay will realize, there are many respects in which my own analysis of totalitarianism differs from that of Finer, contained in his Chapter 3, headed 'The Totalitarian State'.

21 On this question see *Payne,* Chapters x–xv.

22 Considerations of space have precluded discussion of many other countries which are discussed by Finer, and reference should be made to his book. South Africa and Rhodesia are omitted from discussion because they present difficulty of classification—they are, indeed, régimes of a dual nature, in the sense that they combine *both* the democratic features of the polity *and* the autocratic features of colonial or occupying rule. 'A relatively narrow but absolutely large body of citizens governs itself by more or less (rather less than more) Liberal-democratic procedures, but governs the remainder of the population in an authoritarian way.' (Based on a private communication from Professor Finer, and quoted with his permission.) It need hardly be said that the use of the term 'totalitarian' as applied to South Africa is completely inaccurate.

23 This was the conclusion reached by Friedrich in 1969 and represents a modification of the view which he first expressed in 1954—see *Friedrich,* 1969, pp. 153–4.

Bibliography

(Much more complete bibliographies will be found in *Friedrich and Brzezinski* and the new work by *Jänicke* which is referred to in footnote 11, Chapter 1.)

To list the entire literature which now exists on totalitarianism would require another book as long as the present one. I have endeavoured to include some of the works which I have found useful and stimulating, and all the books and articles referred to in the footnotes.

ADORNO, THEODOR W., *The Authoritarian Personality* (*Studies in Prejudice*), American Jewish Committee, Social Studies Series No. 3, New York 1950.

ALLEN, J. W., *A History of Political Thought in the 16th Century*, London 1960.

ANDRESKI, STANISLAV, *Parasitism and Subversion. The Case of Latin America*, London 1970.

ANDREWES, A., *The Greek Tyrants*, London 1956.

AQVARONE, ALBERTO, *L'organizzazione dello Stato totalitario*, Torino 1965.

ARENDT, HANNAH, *The Origins of Totalitarianism*, New York 1958.

ARMSTRONG, JOHN A., *The Politics of Totalitarianism: The Communist Party of the Soviet Union from 1934 to the present*, New York 1961.

ARON, RAYMOND, *Democracy and Totalitarianism*, London 1968.

—— *18 Lectures on Industrial Society*, London 1967.

—— *Main Currents in Sociological Thought*, Vol. II, 'Durkheim, Pareto, Weber' trs. Richard Howard, Helen Weaver, London 1968.

AUTY, PHYLLIS, *Tito—A Biography*, London 1970.

AVINERI, SHLOMO, *The Social and Political Thought of Karl Marx*, Cambridge 1968.

BARBER, BENJAMIN R., 'Conceptual Foundations of Totalitarianism' in *Totalitarianism in Perspective. Three views* (Friedrich, Curtis and Barber), London 1969.

BARBER, B. R. and SPIRO, H. J., 'The Concept of "Totalitarianism" as the Foundation of American Counter-Ideology in the Cold War'. American Political Science Association, *Annual Meeting* 1967.

BARKER, ERNEST (trs., intro., notes and appendixes), *The Politics of Aristotle*, Oxford 1946.

BIERSTEDT, ROBERT, *Emile Durkheim*, London 1969.

BINCHY, D. A., *Church and State in Fascist Italy*, London 1941.

BOURDEAUX, MICHAEL, *Patriarch and Prophets. Persecution of the Russian Orthodox Church To-day*, London 1969.

—— *Religious Ferment in Russia. Protestant Opposition to Soviet Religious Policy*, London 1968.

BRACHER, KARL DIETRICH, *The German Dictatorship. The Origins, Structure and Effects of National Socialism*, trs. Jean Steinburg, intro. Peter Gay, London 1970.

BRACHER, K. D., SAUER, WOLFGANG and SCHULZ, GERHARD, *Die National-sozialistische Machtergreifung. Studien zur Errichtung des totalitären Herr-schaftssystems in Deutschland 1933/34*, Köln und Opladen 1960.

BUCHHEIM, HANS, *Totalitäre Herrschaft. Wesen und Merkmale*, Kösel Verlag, München 1962.

────── *Totalitarian Rule: its nature and characteristics*, trans. Ruth Hein, annotations Kurt P. Tauber and Ruth Hein, Middletown, Conn. 1968.

────── 'The S.S.—Instrument of Domination', Part II in *Anatomy of the SS State*, Helmut Krausnick, Hans Buchheim, Martin Broszat, Hans Adolf Jacobsen, London 1968.

BULLOCK, ALAN, *Hitler, a Study in Tyranny* (revised edition), London 1962.

BUONARROTI, F. M., *Conspiration pour l'égalite*. Dite de Babeuf, Books I and II. Preface, Georges Lefebvre, Paris 1957.

BURCH, BETTY (Ed.), *Dictatorship and Totalitarianism. Selected Readings*, New York 1964.

BURROWES, ROBERT, 'Totalitarianism: the Revised Standard Edition', in *World Politics*, Vol. XXI, No. 2, 1969, pp. 272–89.

CALVIN, JOHN, *Institutes of the Christian Religion*, Vols I and II, a new translation by Henry Beveridge, Edinburgh 1868.

────── *The Cambridge Medieval History*, Vol. IV: *The Byzantine Empire*. Part II. 'Byzantism and its Neighbours', ed. J. M. Hussey, Cambridge 1966.

────── *The Cambridge Medieval History*, Vol. IV: *The Byzantine Empire*. Part I. 'Government, Church and Civilization', ed. J. M. Hussey, Cambridge 1967.

CARLYLE, R. W. and A. J., *A History of Medieval Political Theory in the West*, Vol. VI. Second Impression. Edinburgh and London, 1940.

CARSTEN, F. L., *The Rise of Fascism*, London 1967.

CIANO, GALEAZZO, *Ciano's Diary 1937–38*, trs. with notes by Andreas Mayor, Intro. Malcolm Muggeridge, London 1952.

────── *Ciano's Diary 1939–43*, ed. Malcolm Muggeridge, foreword by Sumner Welles, London 1947.

CLAUSEWITZ, CARL VON, *On War*, ed. with an intro. by A. Rapoport, London 1968.

COBBAN, ALFRED, *Rousseau and the Modern State* (Revised edition), London 1964.

COHEN, RONALD and MIDDLETON, JOHN (Eds.), *Comparative Political Systems. Studies in the Politics of Pre-Industrial Socieeist*, New York 1967.

COHN, NORMAN, *The Pursuit of the Millenium. Revolutionary Millenarians and Mystical Anarchists of the Middle Ages*, revised and expanded edition, London 1970.

CONQUEST, ROBERT, *The Great Terror. Stalin's Purge of the 30's*, London 1968.

────── *Cuba and the Rule of Law*, International Commission of Jurists, Geneva 1962.

CONSTANT, BENJAMIN, *De l'Esprit de Conquête et de l'Ursupation dans leurs rapports avec la civilization Européene*, Pleiade edn, Paris 1964.

CURTIS, MICHAEL, 'Retreat from Totalitarianism' in *Totalitarianism in Perspective* (Friedrich, Curtis and Barber), London 1969.

DEAKIN, F. W., *The Brutal Friendship, Mussolini, Hitler and the Fall of Italian Fascism*, London 1962.

DIEHL-THIELE, PETER, *Partei und Staat im Dritten Reich. Untersuchungen zum Verhältnis von NSDAP und allgemeiner innerer Staatsverhaltung 1933–1945*, Munich 1969.

DRATH, MARTIN (see RICHERT, G.).

DURKHEIM, E., *Socialism and Saint-Simon*, trs. Charlotte Sattler, Antioch Press 1958.

D'ENTREVES, A. P., *The Notion of the State. An Introduction to Political Theory*, London 1967.

EHRENBERG, VICTOR, *The Greek State*, New York 1960.

FAINSOD, MERLE, *How Russia is Ruled* (Revised edition), Cambridge, Mass. 1963.

——— *Smolensk under Soviet Rule*, Cambridge, Mass. 1958.

DE FELICE, RENZO, *Mussolini il fascista*. I: *La conquista del potere 1921–1925*, Torino 1966.

——— *Mussolini il fascista*. II: *L'organizzazione dello State fascista 1925–1929*, Torino 1968.

FERMI, LAURA, *Mussolini*, Chicago 1961.

FIGGIS, J. N., 'Political Thought in the Sixteenth Century', in *Cambridge Modern History*, chapter XXII, Vol. III, 1904.

FIJALKOWSKI, JURGEN, *Die Wendung zum Fuhrerstaat. Ideologische Komponenten in der politischen Philosophie Carl Schmitts*, Köln/Opladen 1958.

FINER, S. F., *Comparative Government*, London 1970.

FLERON, F. J. Jr., 'Soviet Area Studies and the Social Sciences: Some methodological problems in Communist Studies', *Soviet Studies*, Jan. 1968, Oxford.

——— 'Toward a Reconceptualization of Political Change in the Soviet Union', *Comparative Politics*, Jan. 1969, New York.

——— (Ed.), *Communist Studies and the Social Sciences: Essays on Methodology and Empirical Theory*, Chicago 1969.

FRAENKEL, ERNEST, *The Dual State. A Contribution to the theory of Dictatorship*, New York 1941.

FRIEDRICH, CARL J., 'The Evolving Theory and Practice of Totalitarian Regimes' in *Totalitarianism in Perspective. Three Views* (Friedrich, Curtis and Barber), London 1969.

——— 'The Unique Character in Totalitarian Society', in *Totalitarianism*, Proceedings of a Conference held at the American Academy of Art and Sciences, March 1953, ed. Carl J. Friedrich, Cambridge, Mass. 1954.

——— 'Totalitarianism: Recent Trends', *Problems of Communism*, May/June 1968 Washington.

FRIEDRICH, CARL J. and BRZEZINSKI, ZBIGNIEW K., *Totalitarian Dictatorship and Autocracy*, 2nd edn, revised New York 1966.

FROMM, ERICH, *The Fear of Freedom*, London 1942.

GALINDEZ, JESUS DE, *La Era de Trujillo*, Santiago de Chile 1956.

GENTILE, GIOVANNI, *Genesis and Structure of Society*, trs. H. S. Harris, Urbana, Illinois 1960.

——— *Che Cosa è il fascismo? Discorsi e polemiche*, Florence 1925.

GOEBBELS, JOSEPH, *The Goebbels Diaries*, ed. Louis P. Lochner, London 1948.

GRAY, JACK (Ed.), *Modern China's Search for a Political Form*, Oxford 1969.

GROSSMANN, KURT R., *Die Unbesungenen Helden*, Berlin 1961.

HAN FEI TZU, *The Complete Works of Han Fei Tzu. A classic of Chinese legalism*, trs. W. K. Liao, London 1939.

HANOVER, HEINRICH and HANNOVER-DRUCK, ELIZABETH, *Politische Justiz 1918–1933. Einleitung: Karl Dietrich Bracher*, Frankfurt 1966.

HARRIS, H. S., *The Social Philosophy of Giovanni Gentile*, Urbana, Illinois 1960.

HART, H. L. A., *Law. Liberty and Morality*, London 1963.

——— *The Concept of Law*, London 1961.

HEGEL, G. F. W., *Hegel's Political Writings*, trs. T. M. Knox. Intro. essay Z. A. Pelczynski, Oxford 1964.

——— *Philosophy of Right*, trs. T. M. Knox, Oxford 1942.

HOBBES, THOMAS, *Leviathan, or the Matter, Form and Power of a Commonwealth Ecclesiastical and Civil*, ed. with an intro. Michael Oakeshott, Oxford 1955.

HUNOLD, ALBERT (Ed.), *Freedom and Serfdom. An Anthology of Western Thought*, Dordrecht, 1961.

HUNT, GEORGE L. and McNEILL, JOHN T. (Eds.), *Calvinism and the Political Order*. Essays prepared for the Woodrow Wilson Lectureship of the National Presbyterian Center, Washington, D.C., Philadelphia 1965.

IONESCU, GHITA, *The Politics of the European Communist States*, London 1967.

JELLINEK, GEORG, *Allgemeine Staatslehre*, 3rd edition by W. Jellinek, Berlin 1922.

JONES, A. H. M., *Sparta*, Oxford 1967.

KAMENKA, E. (Ed.), *A World in Revolution?* The Australian National University lectures 1970, Australia 1970.

KANT, IMMANUEL, *Kant's Political Writings*, edit. with Intro. and notes Hans Reiss, Cambridge 1970.

KANTOROWICZ, HERMANN, 'Dictatorships. A Sociological Study', *Politica*, August 1935, London.

KAROL, K. S., *Guerillas in Power. The Course of the Cuban Revolution*, trs. Arnold Pomerans, London 1971.

KATEB, GEORGE, *Utopia and its Enemies*, New York 1963.

KELSEN, HANS, *Reine Rechtslehre. Einleitung in die Rechtswissenschaftliche Problematik*, Leipzig 1934.

KOHN, HANS, *The Mind of Germany, The Education of a Nation*, London 1961.

KOLARZ, WALTER, *Religion in the Soviet Union*, London 1961.

KORNHAUSER, WILLIAM, *Politics of Mass Society*, London 1960.

KRAUSNICK, HELMUT, BUCHHEIM, HANS, BROSZAT, MARTIN and JACOBSEN, HANS ADOLF, *Anatomy of the S.S. State*. Intro. Elizabeth Wiskemann, London 1968.

KUSIN, VLADIMIR V., *The Intellectual Origins of the Prague Spring. The Development of Reformist Ideas in Czechoslovakia 1956–1967*, Cambridge 1971.

LENIN, V. I., *Collected Works*, Vol. 5. May 1901–1902, trs. Joe Fineberg, George Hanna, ed. Victor Jerome, Moscow 1961. Lawrence & Wishart (Collected Works), London.

———— *Collected Works*, Vol. 31. April/December 1920, trs. Julius Katzer, Moscow 1966. Lawrence & Wishart (Collected Works), London.

LEVY, YVES 'Libertiés formelles, libertés réelles', *Le Contrat Social*, Sept.–Oct. 1966, Paris.

LEWIS, BERNARD, *The Emergence of Modern Turkey*, London 1961.

LEWIS, JOHN WILSON (Ed.), *Party Leadership and Revolutionary Power in China*, Cambridge 1970.

LICHTENBERGER, ANDRÉ, *Le Socialisme au XVIIIᵉ Siècle. Etude sur les Idées Socialistes dans les Ecrivains Français du XVIIIᵉ Siècle avant La Révolution*, Paris 1895.

LIFTON, ROBERT JAY, *Thought Reform and the Psychology of Totalism. A Study of 'Brainwashing' in China*, London 1961.

LIVELY, J. F., *The Enlightenment*. Foreword H. Kearney, London 1966.

LOWENTHAL, RICHARD, *The Totalitarian Revolution of our Time*. Radio Free Europe 1965 (privately circulated).

LUDZ, PETER CHRISTIAN, 'Entwurf einer soziologischen theorie totalitär verfasster Gesellschaft' in *Kölner Zeitschrift für Soziologie und Sozialpsychologie*, Neue Folge der Kölner Vierteljahrshefte für Soziologie, Köln 1964.

———— *Parteielite im Wandel*, Cologne and Opladen 1968.

———— *The German Democratic Republic from the Sixties to the Seventies. A Socio-Political Analysis*. Foreword: Prof. Karl W. Deutsch, Cambridge, Mass. 1970.

MACIVER, R. M., *The Web of Government*, New York 1965.

DE MAISTRE, JOSEPH, *The Works of Joseph de Maistre*. Selected, translated and introduced Jack Lively, London 1965.

MANN, ERIKA, *School for Barbarians. Education under the Nazis*. Intro. Thomas Mann, London 1939.

MANUEL, FRANK E. (Ed.), *Utopias and Utopian Thought. A Timely Appraisal*, Boston 1967.

MARCUSE, HERBERT, *One Dimensional Man, The Ideology of Industrial Society*, London 1964.

—— 'Repressive Tolerance' in Robert Paul Wolff, Barrington Moore Jnr. and Herbert Marcuse, *A Critique of Pure Tolerance*, London 1969, pp. 93–137.

MASON, T. W., 'The Primacy of Politics—Politics and Economics in National Socialist Germany', in S. J. Woolf (ed.), *The Nature of Fascism*, New York 1968, pp. 165–95.

MEDVEDEV, ZHORES and ROY, *A Question of Madness*, trs. Ellen de Kadt, London 1971.

MEINECKE, FRIEDRICH, *Machiavellism. The Doctrine of Raison d'Etat and Its Place in Modern History*, trs. Douglas Scott. General Intro. to Meinecke's work W. Stark, New York 1965.

MINISTRY OF CORPORATIONS—ROME, 'The Development and Work of the Corporate Organization, in the 1st Decennary of Fascism', Rome 1933.

MOLNAR, THOMAS, 'De l'utopie et des utopistes', *Le Contrat Social*, Nov.–Dec. 1966, Paris.

MONTER, E. WILLIAM, *Calvin's Geneva*, New York 1967.

MOORE, BARRINGTON J., Jnr., *Political Power and Social Theory. Six Studies*, Cambridge, Mass. 1958.

—— *Social Origins of Dictatorship and Democracy. Lord and Peasant in the Making of the Modern World*, London 1969.

MORELLY, *Code de la Nature ou le véritable esprit de ses lois, de tout temps négligé méconnu*. Intro. V. P. Volguine, Paris 1953.

MORRIS, WILLIAM, *News from Nowhere or an Epoch of Rest*, ed. James Redmond, London 1970.

MOSCA, GAETANO, *The Ruling Class* (Elementie di Scienza Politica), trs. Hannah D. Kahn, ed. and revised intro. Arthur Livingston, New York 1939.

MOSSE, GEORGE L., *The Crisis of German Ideology. Intellectual Origins of the Third Reich*, London 1966.

MURRA, JOHN V., 'On Inca Political Structure' in *Comparative Political Systems*, ed. Ronald Cohen and John Middleton.

MUSSOLINI, BENITO, 'Day to Day Pamphlets', No. 18. 'The Political and Social Doctrine of Fascism', trs. Jane Soames, London 1933.

—— *Opera Omnia*—36 vols. Ed. Edoardo e Duilio Sushel, Firenze 1952–63.

NEGLEY, GLEN and PATRICK, I. MAX, *The Quest for Utopia. An Anthology of Imaginary Societies*, New York 1962.

NEUMANN, FRANZ, *Behemoth. The Structure and Practice of National Socialism 1933–1944*, New York 1966.

—— *The Democratic and the Authoritarian State. Essays in Political and Legal Theory*, ed. and preface Herbert Marcuse, New York 1964.

NEWMAN, KARL I., *Zeistörung und Selbstzerstörung der Demokratic Europa 1918–1938*, Köln, Berlin 1965.

NICOLAEVSKY, BORIS F., *Power and the Soviet Elite*, 'The Letter of an Old Bolshevik and Other Essays, ed. Janet D. Zagoria, New York 1965.

NIETZSCHE, FRIEDRICH, *The Birth of Tragedy and the Genealogy of Morals*, trs. Francis Golffing, New York 1956.

NOLTE, ERNEST, *Theorien über den Faschismus*, Köln/Berlin 1967.

OAKESHOTT, MICHAEL, 'The Masses in Representative Democracy' in *Freedom and Serfdom*, ed. Albert Hunold, Dordrecht 1961.

O'BRIEN, PATRICK, 'On the Adequacy of the Concept of Totalitarianism', *Studies in Comparative Communism*, Jan. 1970.

ORLOW, DIETRICH, *The History of the Nazi Party 1919–1933*, Pittsburgh 1969.

ORTEGA Y GASSET, JOSÉ, *The Revolt of the Masses*, London 1961.

PARETO, VILFREDO, *Sociological Writings*, intro. S. E. Finer, trans. Derick Mirfin, London 1966.

PARIS, ROBERT, *Histoire du Fascisme en Italie*, Vol. I: 'Des Origines à la prise du parvoir,' Paris 1962.

PATRICK, I. MAX, *The Quest for Utopia. An Anthology of Imaginary Societies*, New York 1962.

PAYNE, STANLEY G., *Falange. A History of Spanish Fascism*, London 1962.

PETERSON, EDWARD N., *The Limits of Hitler's Power*, Princeton, N.J. 1969.

PICKER, DR HENRY, *Hitlers Tischgespräche im Führerhauptquartier*, ed. Gerhard Ritter, Bonn 1951.

PLAMENATZ, JOHN, *Man and Society*, Vol. II: 'A Critical Examination of Some Important Social and Political Theories from Machiavelli to Marx,' London 1963.

POPPER, K. R., *The Open Society and Its Enemies*, Vols. I and 2, revised edn., London 1952.

RICHERT, ERNEST, *Macht Ohne Mandat. Der Staatsapparat in dem Besatzungsgau Deutschlands. Einleitung*, Martin Drath, Köln und Opladen 1958.

RIGBY, T. H., 'New Trends in the Study of Soviet Politics', *Politics*, May 1970.

ROTHFELS, HANS, *The German Opposition to Hitler. An Assessment*, London 1961.

ROUSSEAU, JEAN-JACQUES, *The Social Contract*, trans. and intro. Maurice Cranston, London 1968 (Penguin Classics).

SAINT-JUST (LOUIS-ANTOINE-LÉON), Oeuvres Choisie Discours—Rapports. Institutions Républicaines Proclamations—Lettres, Paris 1968.

SAINT-SIMON ET D'ENFANTIN, *Oeuvres*, 47 vols., Paris 1865–78.

SCHAPIRO, L., *Rationalism and Nationalism in Russian Nineteenth-Century Thought*, New Haven and London 1967.

——— *The Origin of the Communist Autocracy. Political Opposition in the Soviet State, 1st Phase 1917–1922*, London 1955.

——— 'The Concept of Totalitarianism', *Survey*, no. 73, Autumn 1969.

——— *The Communist Party of the Soviet Union* (2nd edition, revised and enlarged), London 1970.

——— 'The Roles of the Monolithic Party under the Totalitarian Leader', in *Party Leadership and Revolutionary Power in China*, ed. J. W. Lewis, Cambridge 1970.

SCHMITT, CARL, *Über die drei Arten des Rechtswissenschaftlichen Denkens*, Hamburg 1934.

SCHURMANN, FRANZ, *Ideology and Organization in Communist China*, 2nd ed. (enlarged), Berkeley 1968.

SETON-WATSON, HUGH, *Neither War Nor Peace, The Struggle for Power in the Post-War World*, London 1960.

SIEDEL, RYMO and JENKNER, SIEGFRIED, *Wege der Totalitarismus-Forschung*, Darmstadt 1968.

SKILLING, H. GORDON and GRIFFITHS, FRANKLYN (Eds.), *Interest Groups in Soviet Politics*, Princeton 1971.

SKINNER, B. F., *Walden Two*, New York 1948.

SMITH, DENIS MACK, *Italy. A Modern History*, Ann Arbor, Michigan 1959.

SOREL, GEORGES, *Reflections on Violence*, trs. T. E. Hulme, J. Roth. Intro. Edward A. Shils, New York 1961.

SPEER, ALBERT, *Memoirs. Inside the Third Reich*, trs. from the German by Richard and Clara Winston. Intro. Eugene Davidson, London 1970.

SPIRO, H. J. and BARBER, B. R., 'The Concept of "Totalitarianism" as the Foundation of American Counter-Ideology in the Cold War', *American Political Science Association Annual Meeting* 1967.

STAFF, ILSE, *Justiz im Dritten Reich. Eine Dokumentation*, Frankfurt 1964.

STEPHEN, JAMES FITZJAMES, *Liberty, Equality, Fraternity*, ed. R. J. White, Cambridge 1967.

STERN, FRITZ, *The Politics of Cultural Despair. A Study in the Rise of the Germanic Ideology*, New York 1965.

STORRY, RICHARD, *A History of Modern Japan*, Harmondsworth 1960.

SUAREZ, ANDRÉS, *Cuba: Castroism and Communism, 1959–1966*, foreword Ernst Halperin, Cambridge, Mass. and London 1967.

SUETONIUS, *The Twelve Caesars*, trs. Robert Graves, Harmondsworth 1967.

TALMON, J. L., *Political Messianism. The Romantic Phase*, London 1960.

—— *The Origins of Totalitarian Democracy*, London 1952.

THIBON, GUSTAVE, *Nietzsche ou Le Déclin de L'Esprit*, Paris 1948.

THUCYDIDES, *The Peloponnesian War*, trs. Rex Warner, Harmondsworth 1954.

TOCQUEVILLE, ALEXIS DE, *Oeuvres, Papiers et Correspondances*, Vol. 1: *De La Démocratie en Amerique* (in two volumes), Intro. Harold J. Laski, Paris 1951.

TREVOR-ROPER, H. R., *The Last Days of Hitler*, London 1947.

TUAN SHENG, CH'IEN, *The Government and Politics of China 1912–1949*, Stanford 1950.

TUCKER, ROBERT C., *The Soviet Political Mind. Studies in Stalinism and Post-Stalin Change*, New York 1963.

VIERECK, PETER, *Conservatism Revisited*, New York 1965.

WAELDER, ROBERT, 'Characteristics of Totalitarianism', *Psychoanalytic Study of Society*, 1960.

WEBER, MAX, *Wirtschaft und Gesellschaft. Studienausgabe*, ed. Johann Winckelmann, Köln/Berlin 1956.

WILLMS, BERNARD, *Die totale Freiheit. Fichtes Politische Philosophie*, Köln and Opladen 1967.

WILSON, LAWRENCE (trs.), *The Road to Dictatorship in Germany 1918–1933. A Symposium by German Historians*, London 1964.

WITTFOGEL, KARL A., *Oriental Despotism. A Comparative Study of Total Power*, New Haven 1957.

WOLFE, BERTRAM D., *Communist Totalitarianism. Key to the Soviet System*, Boston 1956.

WOLFE, ROBERT PAUL, MOORE, BARRINGTON, Jnr. and MARCUSE, HERBERT, *A Critique of Pure Tolerance*, London 1969.

WOOLF, S. J. (Ed.), *The Nature of Fascism*, New York 1968.

Index

142/*Index*

Key Concepts in Political Science
GENERAL EDITOR: Leonard Schapiro
EXECUTIVE EDITOR: Peter Calvert

Other titles in the same series include:

ALREADY PUBLISHED

IN PREPARATION

Totalitarianism